How to Become Data Literate

The Basics for Educators

Second Edition

Susan Rovezzi Carroll
David Carroll

ROWMAN & LITTLEFIELD PUBLISHERS, INC
Lanhan • Boulder • New York • London

Published by Rowman & Littlefield
A wholly owned subsidiary of The Rowman & Littlefield Publishing Group, Inc.
4501 Forbes Boulevard, Suite 200, Lanham, Maryland 20706
www.rowman.com

Unit A, Whitacre Mews, 24-36 Stannary Street, London SE11 4AB

British Library Cataloguing in Publication Information Available

Library of Congress Cataloging-in-Publication Data Available

ISBN 978-1-4758-1331-9 (hardcover)
ISBN 978-1-4758-1332-6 (paperback)
ISBN 978-1-4758-1333-3 (e-book)

♾™ The paper used in this publication meets the minimum requirements of American National Standard for Information Sciences—Permanence of Paper for Printed Library Materials, ANSI/NISO Z39.48-1992.

Printed in the United States of America

To Polly Fitz, a pioneer and champion. One of the first female deans at the University of Connecticut, she demanded the practice of leadership, articulated the importance of diversity, and continuously practiced a generosity of spirit.

Contents

Preface

No Child Left Behind and subsequent state legislation and regulation have imposed seemingly overwhelming accountability requirements on public PreK-12 educators. In order to fulfill these requirements, public schools collect an inordinate amount of data: achievement data (teacher tests, state tests, and standardized tests), attendance data (both teacher and student), teacher credential data, graduation rate data, enrollment data, demographic data, student behavior data, etc. To add another layer of complexity, these data are collected at the student, school, district, and state levels. Collecting the data is often not the problem, although this process should not be minimized. More often, problems occur when trying to figure out what to do with the data.

The phrase "data-driven decision making" has become the mantra for solving all problems related to public education. Oftentimes, however, educators have not been adequately trained in how to use data to gain information or to solve a problem. Consequently, using the available data to complete reports, solve problems, and answer questions seems an insurmountable task to many educators.

This book makes major strides toward addressing this issue. Not only does it speak in language everyone can understand, it focuses on understanding research and statistics from a conceptual point of view, rather than mathematically and formulaic. In other words, it strives to make educators data literate. Data literacy requires professionals to be able to understand and analyze their data as well as to communicate any findings necessary for solving problems or directing future programs. For those without degrees in statistics, which includes most people, it is much more important to understand which statistic to use to answer which question, how to ask the question, and how to interpret the results of any analysis. Of little-to-no consequence to educators are the mathematical formulae for analyzing the data.

Chapter 1 clarifies the language of research and statistics and explains the true value of statistics to educators inundated with data. Chapters 5 and 6 untangle the topics of sampling and hypotheses, two areas that have been known to confuse some of the most astute researchers. Chapters 2–10 describe, explain, and demystify the analyses used to address the most frequent questions educators are called upon to answer in their efforts to improve student achievement and reform public education. Using examples familiar to educators, the authors explain a variety of analyses showing how to compare scores for different groups of students, or how to compare pretest and posttest scores, and how to determine, for example, if the Iowa Tests will predict how well students will do on state-designed tests, common questions asked by educators. The final chapter explains how to present results for the intended audience, which, for public school PreK-12 educators, is generally not comprised of academics reading peer-reviewed articles in journals. Rather, it is for administrators, school boards, and community members. Among other strategies, the authors stress the need to use graphs and other diagrams that are visually pleasing and easily understood.

Because this book is designed for educated professionals that must use, analyze, and translate data for the general populous, it is different from most books on statistics. In the long run, this book is intended to underscore the value and potential of data and develop data-literate educators. Decisions based on excellent data produce meaningful action strategies that benefit the schools and their entire range of stakeholders including students, parents, staff, and the community at large. Hopefully, the reader will not only understand the use of statistics better after reading this book, but will also enjoy using statistics.

Introduction

The Compelling Case for Data Literacy

The potential to influence public education beyond any public school reform initiative comes down to one word: *data*. Educators are beginning to use data to track student performance in their classrooms, achievement trends in their schools, curricula and program impact, staffing needs, space and resource allocation, and fiscal expenditures in their systems. They are also using data to make choices concerning effective instructional methods, academic interventions, student behavior strategies, and management approaches intended to positively impact their schools. The options for collecting, aggregating, and interpreting data for use in school improvement initiatives are steadily increasing.

Historically, public schools have had access to volumes of data. Despite this wealth of data, decision-making in school districts has been based on frequency counts of raw data, or the averaging of standardized test scores on the aggregate level. At worst, it has relied on hunches and best guesses. The data were rarely used to guide, drive, and improve instruction at the classroom level.

Everyday life in schools presents educators with all types of data. Superintendents review data for assessing student performance and outcomes. Principals rely on data to evaluate teacher effectiveness and the efficacy of academic or social-behavioral interventions. Teachers assess student performance both formatively and summatively to guide, improve, and track instruction. Boards of Education make critical data-based decisions about what to keep and what to cut in school budgets. Today, many states have added on Common Core State Standards in the trail of No Child Left Behind, which mentioned research 216 times. Both initiatives stress the imperative that data must be used effectively.

Now more than ever, educators are being held accountable by taxpayers, students, parents, government officials, and the business community for supportable documentation of educational results. To be responsive to their stakeholders, school districts have been struggling to align the reporting of their data with information expectations. Data is now everyone's job and everyone's concern.

Yet let's face it. The image of "data" suffers. First, for many highly degreed educators, data conjures up memories of unpopular graduate requirements in research methods or statistics courses. Second, data management requires time. It is labor intensive at a time when educators cannot find an extra minute in their day. Third, many educators are uncertain about their abilities to manage data, accurately analyze quantitative findings, and interpret the results. For many, their graduate school classes in research design and statistics were mathematically difficult, highly technical, and lacked real application to their day-to-day lives in a school setting.

School databases are jam-packed with standard-based test scores, SAT results, assessments of reading and math programs, faculty and staff profiles, demographic and enrollment data, classroom performance assessments, student discipline patterns, attendance and dropout rates. These data can be massaged to produce a host of statistics with just the click of the mouse. In fact, the terms *data mining* and *drilling down* have become commonly accepted jargon along with the mantras *research-based practice* or *data-based decision making.* Many schools have rushed to purchase data warehousing technology but the training to use it correctly and even more importantly, to disaggregate data, are sorely missing. Without the foundation of a knowledge base, the use of computer software and data management technology can provide schools with risky mis-information that can have serious consequences.

The ingression of data has exposed a raw nerve. The lack of comfort that many educators have in working with data poses a great challenge as school districts make the transition from a data rich to an information rich environment. To some extent, software technology has provided the automobile without a course in driver education. How many educators will admit that their million-dollar data warehouse system is barely touched? Despite the increased amount of data that are available, many educators continue to feel uncomfortable when tasked to analyze and to use student data effectively.

Data literacy is the solution. It is clear that educators need to build their knowledge base for how to develop, manipulate, and interpret data. More specifically, this means having the ability to formulate and answer questions using data as part of evidence-based thinking, selecting and using appropriate data tools, interpreting information from data, evaluating evidence-based differences, using data to solve real problems and communicating solutions.

Educators will need *data literacy* to transform their data into powerhouses of information. To do this they will need to use data correctly, judiciously, and strategically.

It boils down to becoming data literate.

The good news is that educators know what questions they want answered.

- Are reading scores similar across elementary schools in the district?
- Has classroom math performance for fourth graders improved from their third grade performance?
- Are preschoolers from all neighborhoods kindergarten-ready?
- How can students' reading performance be modified for differentiated instruction?
- Are the numbers of students on meal subsidies increasing significantly?
- Should we adopt a new math curriculum and discard the old?
- Has the behavior management program reduced discipline referrals and suspensions?
- What is the level of parent satisfaction with our elementary schools?
- Did the new mathematics module increase math skills?
- What are our teacher retention rates and how do they compare with our peers?
- How did our college bound cohort perform on freshman grade point average?
- What effect does the new language arts curriculum have on writing?
- What is the demographic profile of students who score "below basic" proficiency?
- Is the referral rate to special education increasing among children of color?
- What impact do the after school programs have on school attendance rates?

However, the fundamental statistical knowledge needed to "separate the wheat from the chaff" and produce the information required to answer these difficult questions remains a mystery for many educators.

These educators have content that is well grounded; but the methodology aligned to the content is needed to use data correctly, effectively, and strategically. Here are a few of the methodological concepts that are challenging to most educators.

- When should I use the median instead of the mean?
- How can I accurately present my data with graphing techniques?
- What piece of information does variability provide?
- What is the difference among nominal, ordinal, and interval scales?

- How do I state the research and null hypotheses?
- What are independent and dependent variables?
- What can I do to avoid errors in my results?
- Why should I choose a probability level of .01 instead of .05?
- Do I need to test all first graders or just a sample of classrooms?
- How can I document that pre and post gains are significant?
- When should I use a t-test instead of ANOVA?
- How do I know if a correlation documents a strong relationship?
- Can rubric scores be compared by classroom with a chi-square analysis?
- How can I report my results from data in an accurate, clear, and powerful manner?

To become data literate, educators need three requisite skills:

- the ability to frame questions so that the statistics can be manipulated to provide answers;
- the ability to disaggregate data to address specific rather than global issues;
- the ability to assess the value *and* implications of reports that are data-based.

Most important, the foundation of a data literacy skill set rests on a working knowledge of statistical concepts and research methodology.

The ultimate purpose of this book is to help educators to become data literate and for schools to make the transition from being data rich to information rich. More immediately, this book is intended to be a user-friendly, educator's primer, presenting the statistical and research basics of what you need to develop the three requisite skills of data literacy. It presents concepts in a simple and immediately applicable manner. It makes data comprehensible and accessible.

By focusing on conceptual applications versus statistical theory, this book will leave the reader with the confident attitude that "I can do this." In the long run, this book is intended to underscore the magnificence of data. Decisions based on excellent data produce meaningful action strategies that benefit the school and its entire range of stakeholders including students, parents, staff, and the community at large.

Chapter One

Speaking the Language Correctly

Few educators eagerly anticipate taking a research or statistics course. Many times there is a knowledge gap between high school mathematics and the quantitative courses of graduate study. For some, math was a course in high school taken primarily as a college application requirement. As a result, not much more than Math 101 is taken in college. For others, the image of statistics was, and remains, formula-driven, and thus intricately complex and intimidating. Some of those brave souls who took a statistics course at the undergraduate level most likely had their preconceptions confirmed by professors who taught the subject from a computational perspective. Consequently, many students were likely alienated from pursuing graduate level study that included this important and useful field.

This book is not a statistics text. It is a primer for educators who want to use data to help them fully understand their students, their schools, and school districts. In this book statistics is presented as a way of thinking. It is a logical, simplified way of using data to present information in a strategic manner. Hopefully, the discussion will present the enormous benefits of embracing data.

WHAT ARE STATISTICS?

Look at the data set in Figure 1.1 that represents pre and post performance test scores for 28 students. It can make your head spin. What can you tell about overall student performance from "eyeballing" the data set?

- Are most children performing well or performing poorly?
- What is the typical score for the majority of students?

```
001 2221222132111211120102120201110201111121 0122011221011
002 1311113131112300301113113111110133312132 1111101110110
003 3221322132212210202021030 2120200120021 0312000200110
004 3330333123300320002032020 2130300120021 0103000300031
005 2211221323211211201122112 2311211122021 2312011211111
006 1221122111111211211212121111111101111021 1111001211111
007 2221222123311210203211313011313200210121 1212000310211
008 2211221112210211101122212012112101211211 311010211122
009 3331332123210220310021303 2130203130033 0303000320030
010 3330333033200320303133103 2230200020031 0201000220021
011 3210322132210210201032202010211200110011 1111011111111
012 3331332033210320302032313 3330311110032 0313001220121
013 3330323132200310313031303 2331100120021 0312001220130
014 1201221102211202102011023013301103100310031 0012001120111
015 2221222122200210213130102011313200331010 0313001220011
016 1310321232100101300031130313321103110111 0321001310101
017 2201221032021201211123123110101210013100131 1111030203101
019 2330232023312313302121203011202112301211 0303010210011
020 3200120133101100201021020010011003010100313001010131
021 2221332033210311212032220202210300121130 1313002330030
022 2320322112310320212131102011212002110211213000110031
023 3321312213310100300130002111212100310210321031332300
024 3320232022300320301032303020303000100230302000110021
025 1211222122311211312111211112122111111121 2212101111211
026 2220232013201330111121201120101110111 0311001110131
027 2331223032301302302112221123102122102110122011122210
028 2331222112201210201122212021202101211211112001221121
```

**Figure 1.1.   Data Set: Pre and Post Performance Scores for 28
Students**

- Were the instructional techniques employed this year effective?
- If students are making gains—to what degree?
- Are students from different classrooms performing the same?
- Are segments of students (boys and girls) performing differently?
- How does performance compare with other schools in the system or the region?

Most of us cannot answer these questions by reviewing a set of data. Even the small set of 28 pre and post performance scores displayed in Figure 1.1 is incomprehensible. Our human minds are limited in their capacity to absorb a set of numbers, retain them, process them, and then make sense of them in interpretation.

Statistics is an area of math that seeks to make order out of a diverse collection of facts. With a single number, statistics can summarize the properties of large groups of numbers. They help us to obtain an understanding of our data. Statistical techniques summarize data making complex masses of numbers simple. By using them, we are able to crunch large sets of numbers into usable and actionable information.

Basically, statistics should be thought of as numbers that summarize the properties of large groups of numbers. If you have been given a massive assortment of number and have no hope of understanding them, although you have looked at them for hours, use statistics. Life will become less complicated. How great would that be?

THE BENEFITS OF USING STATISTICS

Essentially there are three benefits of using statistics. These will be the focus of this book.

1. *To summarize information and present it in a straightforward, compelling manner.* Some statistics called "measures of central tendency" allow *one* number to indicate the central message of a group of scores. A singular number can tell us how our students performed in the set of test data in Figure 1.1. This is of great value to educators. The measures (means, medians, and modes) are used often to make decisions. Another type of statistic is used to qualify the message of central tendency. It is called "variability" and it can show how much dispersion or spread there is in your data set of scores. Again, from a single number we can tell if our students are performing similarly or disparately to each other, to students in the same grade levels, across other schools in our district, in the region, state, and even across the nation. (This ability may become even more valuable with the move toward Common Core State Standards in many states across the country.) Without these two types of statistics, the performance test scores in Figure 1.1 cannot tell us much. They only have value when statistical techniques are applied to them.

2. *To tell us whether something we did had an impact and was worthwhile, so that we can take action.* Statistics are used to provide empirical evidence upon which we can make sound decisions. They tell us how seriously we should regard differences among sets of student scores. Did gains in performance occur by chance or are they statistically significant? What instructional technique works best with a given group of students? Did the new curriculum make a difference? What impact did our policy have? Should we maintain the status quo or make a change? Should this curriculum be modified, and if so, in what way? Educators can make smart choices with just a few simple statistical techniques such as t-tests, One-Way Analysis of Variance procedures, and chi-square analysis. These will be discussed in this primer.

3. *To document relationships that are meaningful so that we can take action.* Correlation statistics can tell us whether two events are related, and to

what degree. Similar to the previously stated purpose, we can use these data to make decisions and to take action. For example, what is the relationship between hours of after school remedial help and student performance on classroom tests? Do students who are tardy get suspended more often? Is having breakfast related to reading readiness? Is parent involvement in your school related to types of logistical support (childcare, transportation)? What impact does our secondary school program have on subsequent college preparedness?

For educators, data literacy is an imperative. Today, data are relied upon more often and from more stakeholders of public education. To correctly provide answers, educators must be comfortable in determining what data are needed and then collecting, ordering, sorting, categorizing, summarizing, manipulating and reporting what is compiled. Statistics can make the process smooth and ultimately make life easy for the most critical step—interpreting what you find out. This will be the basis for smart decisions and action steps in your school settings.

GENERAL CLASSIFICATIONS OF DATA: QUANTITATIVE AND QUALITATIVE

Statistics involves collecting information called data, analyzing it, and making meaningful decisions based on it. Collected data, which represent observations or measurements of something of interest, can be classified into two general types: qualitative and quantitative.

- *Qualitative data* refers to observations that are descriptive. These data represent categories. This might include demographic data such as gender, ethnicity/race, socioeconomic status, household composition, school location (rural, urban, and suburban), school type (elementary, middle, and secondary).

- *Quantitative data* represent various observations or measurements that are numerical, such as classroom performance, number of students on free/reduced lunch, school attendance rates, *Smarter Balanced* results, library usage, kindergarten enrollment data, parent satisfaction, SAT performance, and others.

THE ESSENTIAL COMPONENT IN DATA: VARIABLES

Data are derived from characteristics about individuals, objects, or events. These characteristics are called *variables*. Anything that varies and can be measured is called a variable. Variables can be quantitative or qualitative. We attach numbers to our variables in an effort to measure them and apply statistics to them.

Variables such as high school grade point average, age, ethnicity/race, school attendance, college placement, teacher satisfaction, parental support, student suspensions, household composition, homework completion, school climate, program enrollment (special education, gifted/talented), school image, bullying, student attitudes, math achievement, bus transportation, instructional budgets, and teacher retention are a few of the many variables we can measure in education.

Variables that are qualitative are called *categorical* variables. They have different categories and each category takes on a whole number or integer to represent it. For example, school type would be a categorical variable. For some school systems it might have three categories:

$$1 = \text{Elementary}$$
$$2 = \text{Middle}$$
$$3 = \text{Secondary}$$

The variable of gender has two categories: males and females. Males can be assigned a "1" and females a "2," or vice versa.

Variables that are quantitative are classified as either *discrete* or *continuous*. If they are discrete, they can take on only whole numbers or integers. For example, discrete variables might include household size, classroom size, total number of special education students, SAT scores, annual suspensions, or faculty absences. These are represented by whole numbers. If they are continuous variables, they can take on fractions or decimals. Grade reporting, chronological age, reading level, and high school GPA are examples of continuous variables where GPA, for example, might be 3.27. A chart is presented in Figure 1.2 to simplify the classification for data and variables.

All educational variables are measurable or they would not be called variables. We have to assign numbers to all of our variables in order to apply statistics to them. In order to do this we have to understand the scales of measurement. This is essential. Unfortunately, it is an area that is largely misunderstood. If measurement scales are used incorrectly, the wrong statistical technique will be applied to the data. This will yield erroneous information. If a decision or action step is built upon poor information, this creates a problem that could be expensive, embarrassing, and even detrimental to the well being of your school system, your schools, and the students.

Qualitative Data	Categorical Variables	Whole numbers only	Types of Schools: Elementary (1) Middle (2) Secondary (3)
Quantitative Data	Discrete Variables	Whole numbers only	Class Size: 30, 25, 15
	Continuous Variables	Fractions and decimals	Grade Point Average: 3.29 2.33

Figure 1.2. Classification Chart for Data and Variables

FOUR MEASUREMENT SCALES

Whatever exists does so in some amount and can be measured. *Measurement* involves quantifying people, objects, or events on their characteristics. When we collect information about people, objects, and events, we must turn that information into numbers so that we can measure it and make deductions about what we find out. We must express it in numbers not just descriptive phrases.

We cannot claim that our school system has a good organizational climate, or high performance on standards-based tests, or declining absenteeism, or increased faculty competence related to Common Core State Standards, or excellent college placement rates unless we measure or apply numbers to these perceptions. We have to give substance to these allegations. Data can do the job for you.

Because measurement entails quantifying people, objects, or events on their characteristics, you must assign numbers to variables. There are four scales of measurement used to assign numbers to variables. Each is differentiated according to their degree of *precision*. For example, a school nurse might measure a child's general health by level of physical activity, nutritional practices, and taking their temperature. The latter is the most precise measure although all three can provide information about the same variable—health.

There are four measurement scales that are used often in educational settings: nominal, ordinal, internal, and ratio.

NOMINAL MEASUREMENT SCALES

The first measurement scale in the hierarchy is the *nominal* scale. The term "nominal" means to name. The properties of nominal scales are:
• Data categories are mutually exclusive.
• Data categories have no logical order.

Observations are simply classified into categories and assigned a number with no relationship existing between or among the categories. It classifies without ordering. The variable *Homework Completion* can be nominally scaled with a number of either 1 (*complete*) or 0 (*incomplete)* categories. Another example is the variable of *School Attendance*; it would have nominal scaling—*present* or *absent*.

The numeric values could be any combination. Three possibilities for nominal coding of the same variable such as *School Location* are presented in Figure 1.3.

Option 1		Option 2		Option 3	
Variable	**Numbers Assigned**	**Variable**	**Numbers Assigned**	**Variable**	**Numbers Assigned**
Rural	1	Rural	2	Rural	3
Urban	2	Urban	3	Urban	2
Suburban	3	Suburban	1	Suburban	1

Figure 1.3. Three Nominal Scale Options for the Variable of School Location

There is no logical ordering of the categories. Numbers are assigned to the categories, but no quantitative meaning is assigned to the numbers. The numbers mean absolutely *nothing.* We are simply using the numbers to classify people, objects, and events. The numbers we assign to those categories have no ordering, no ranking, no "higher than," no "lower than," no "more of," no "less than" associated with them. They are what their name suggests—nominal, a name to identify. The numbers we assign to our variables in their categories are not quantifiable except to count them up. The total number of males we have will be how many we add up with the value we have assigned to it of either 1 or 2. This is important to note when you are calculating statistics.

There are two basic requirements for nominal measurement:

1. All members of one category must be assigned the same numeral.
2. No two categories are assigned the same numeral.

Some nominally scaled variables have only two categories. These are called *dichotomous* variables. This means that only two numbers can be assigned to each of the categories, respectively. Some examples of dichotomous variables may include language spoken at home (English/Spanish), parent (father/mother), staff (teacher/paraeducator), student (special education/ general education), college placement (accepted/rejected), teacher (tenured/ not tenured), and many others. You may use two numbers (such as 1 and 2 or 0 and 100 or 200 and 300) as the nominal scaling applied to each category.

Nominal scaling is ideal to categorize the schools in our system. *Type of school* the child attends might be categorized as elementary (1), middle (2), and secondary (3). Or, if we have 5 elementary schools, we could nominally scale all 7 of the schools that the children in our town attend as follows in Figure 1.4:

Schools in the school system	Number Assigned
Torringford Elementary School	1
Southwest Elementary School	2
Forbes Elementary School	3
East Elementary School	4
Vogel Wetmore Elementary School	5
Torrington Middle School	6
Torrington High School	7

Figure 1.4.   Nominal Scale for a Seven School System with Five Elementary Schools

Being able to nominally scale our variables this way allows us to *drill down* our data or inspect our data much more thoroughly. Think about how much information you would miss if you had to consolidate all the schools together instead of separating them out by individual categories. With nominal scaling you can drill down by district or by school or by grade or by classroom—to obtain the following information:

- What does math performance look like by classroom in our elementary school?
- How many new students does each school in our system have at the start of the school year?
- What are the ethnic/racial breakdowns by school district in our state?
- Has the proportion of students requiring subsidized lunches changed in our district?

- Are there differences in numbers of students with disabilities across schools?
- How many different languages are spoken in our school district?
- Which school has the most suspensions, and has the percentage changed from last year?

One pitfall threatens. Many individuals get confused about what the actual variable is and what are the respective categories. Sometimes, educators think the *variable* is female or male instead of gender with two categories. This differentiation is very important especially when you are investigating statistical differences with independent and dependent variables, which will be discussed later in the book. Ask yourself: What variable are the individual categories representing? The answer should be the variable itself and not its categories.

ORDINAL MEASUREMENT SCALES

The second type of scaling in the measurement hierarchy is called *ordinal* where there is relative ranking and ordering of an attribute in different categories. There is "more than" and "less than," "higher than" and "lower than," "least of" and "most of." There is a qualitative relationship among numbers in the ordinal scale. Unlike nominal scaling, the numbers in ordinal scales have meaning. Ordinal scales give more information and more precise data than nominal scales do. Here are three examples of ordinal-scaled variables.

Variable: Frequency
Never (1) Rarely (2) Sometimes (3) Frequently (4) Always (5)

Variable: Satisfaction
Dissatisfied (1) Satisfied (2) Very Satisfied (3)

Variable: Program Attainment
Below Expectations (1) Meets Expectations (2) Exceeds Expectations (3)

The properties of ordinal scales are:

- Data categories are mutually exclusive.
- Data categories have some logical order.

- Data categories are scaled according to the amount of a particular characteristic they possess.

One of the most common uses of ordinal scaling is with ratings, preferences, rankings, goal attainment, satisfaction, degrees of quality, and agreement levels—typical of the Likert scales on questionnaires. In today's classroom, teachers often use ordinal scaling for formative assessment of student performance. Table 1.1 is an example of ordinal scaling using a rubric to measure student performance on geometric measurement.

Table 1.1.

Geometric Measurement	Numbers Assigned
Beginning	1
Developing	2
Proficient	3
Advanced	4

As a note, it is helpful to assign your numbers in ordinal scaling in ways that make sense. A rating of "excellent" can have a value of 5 or a value of 1. It is relatively arbitrary. However, it makes more conceptual sense that a low rating with a value of 1 should be assign to a low rating—"poor" whereas, a high rating (5) should be assigned to a high rating—"excellent." After you tabulate your data, it is easier to interpret what you have found out if you assign your ordinal numbers in gradations that make sense.

Another example of ordinal scaling that is used often in education is applied to "Agreement" statements. There are five responses that could be assigned ordinal values. Again, it makes more conceptual sense to assign the value "1" to the least amount of agreement—"Strongly Disagree" and vice versa. Higher levels of agreement should be reflected in the values assigned—5 = "Strongly Agree" (Table 1.2). Again, this is arbitrary.

INTERVAL AND RATIO MEASUREMENT SCALES

There are two *metric* scales of measurement. They are called *interval* and *ratio* scales. Because of their metric nature, these two measurement scales afford the most precise data. With both there are equal intervals or units between any two consecutive numbers. The only difference between interval and ratio scales is the role of zero (0). In interval scales zero is

Table 1.2.

Parent Survey	Numbers Assigned
Strongly Disagree	1
Disagree	2
Undecided/Uncertain	3
Agree	4
Strongly Agree	5

artificial rather than real. Some standardized tests have a zero (0), but it is artificially created rather than real. In ratio scales, zero is real. It signifies the absence of the variable under study. Ratio scales are used often in the biological and physical sciences for variables such as weight, height, calories, and so forth. Interval scales are used more often in disciplines such as education.

Standards-based tests, aptitude tests, achievement tests, intelligence tests, attitude tests, some vocational tests, and many other assessment tools rely on the metric-based measurement scales. When we use data compiled from attendance rates, dropout rates, graduation rates, suspension rates, special education referral rates, and other compilations of data we are reporting our data using these measurement scales.

Because it is possible to assign real numbers to our variables, we can compare our data with other sets of data from similar classrooms, schools, the district, states, regions, the nation, and even other countries. With these two scales we can compute high-level, sophisticated statistics called parametric statistics, discussed later in the book.

The properties of *interval* scales are:

- Data categories are mutually exclusive.
- Data categories have a definite logical order.
- Data categories are scaled according to the amount of a particular characteristic they possess.
- Equal differences in the characteristics are represented by equal differences in the numbers assigned to the categories.
- The point zero (0) is just another point on the scale.

For interval scales, the distance between the numbers 2 and 3 and between 4 and 5 are exactly the same. This is different from ordinal scales where we cannot claim for certain that the distance between good (3) and fair (2) is exactly the same as between poor (1) and fair (2). We assign numbers in ordinal scales, but the distance is not in exact intervals. With interval scales, there is the ordering that is found in ordinal scales, but now we have exact units of measurement.

Interval scales have a zero (0) point in them, but it is arbitrary. Good examples are the interval scales used for temperature—Fahrenheit and Celsius. The difference between 15°C and 20°C is 5°C. The same is true for Fahrenheit. But there is no absence of temperature. The zero is an arbitrary point in both scales.

Ratio scaling is similar to interval scaling in terms of equivalent values between numbers. The only difference is that in ratio scales a zero (0) means something important. It means the absence of whatever the scale is measuring. This type of scaling is encountered more commonly in the physical sciences where there can really be "none"—weight, time, height, calories, or wherever zero is real not artificially created.

The properties of ratio scales are:

• Data categories are mutually exclusive.
• Data categories have a definite logical order.
• Data categories are scaled according to the amount of a particular characteristic they possess.
• Equal differences in the characteristics are represented by equal differences in the numbers assigned to the categories.
• The point zero (0) reflects absence of the characteristic.

CHAPTER SUMMARY

As a summary of the four measurement scales, they can be remembered by the following characteristics.

• *Nominal*—numbers are assigned without order.
• *Ordinal*—numbers are assigned with order but without equal intervals between them.
• *Interval*—numbers are assigned with order and equal units.
• *Ratio*—numbers are assigned with order, equal units, and a true zero point.

When educators are setting up their data, they must know the information covered in this first chapter. It is the foundation of being data literate. Knowing what the differences are in measurement scales, selecting the correct measurement scales for variables, and identifying which ones you use for different statistical procedures are significant steps in setting up data for actionable decisions. This understanding is vital; the use of statistical procedures depends on this basic knowledge.

Chapter Two

Creating a Snapshot of Data
with a Picture

Oftentimes, when we look at a set of data, it is basically a blur of numbers. This is easily addressed by displaying data with a method to the madness. There are several steps that educators should follow when they are working with data sets.

The first step is simply organizing your data. An unordered set of scores is inconvenient for work. Many individuals skip this step because it is elementary and seems too simple to be useful. It is advised that you take the time to organize your data. Doing this will help you to understand the data and to make preliminary conclusions. Equally important, you will be familiarized with the data to the point where no oversights can be uncovered, potentially embarrassing you and minimizing the value of your work.

FREQUENCY DISTRIBUTIONS

When a set of data is presented to you, one of the most useful expenditures of time is to construct a *frequency distribution*. This is systematic arrangement of numerical values from the highest to the lowest—with a count of the number of times each value was obtained. This is a procedure for organizing and summarizing data into a meaningful representation. It does not tell you everything about your information, but it provides a beginning, a convenient way of grouping data so that meaningful patterns can be found.

The first step in developing a frequency distribution is to put all of your scores in order from the lowest value to the highest value. Put them in a column format. Then, use slash marks or *tally* marks beside every score in your column each time it occurs. Some scores may occur only once and some may occur more often. This is why tallies are helpful. Lastly, count up the tally marks and place a real number beside them that shows the frequency that each value occurred in your distribution. This information in chart form can make sense of a set of numbers that appears to be a jumble at first glance.

There are symbols that are typically used. When we set up our frequency distributions, the lowercase letter "x" indicates our scores and the lowercase letter "f" indicates the frequency of occurrence.

For example, let's say your SAT Verbal data looks like the set shown in Figure 2.1.

699	459	450	450	445
420	420	420	420	420
430	420	445	435	467
420	320	420	320	420
689	445	479	450	467
435	430	430	430	420
420	467	467	450	435
320	320	320	320	420
430	445	430	435	467
420	420	320	420	420

Figure 2.1.   Data Set of SAT Verbal Scores for 50 Students

HOW TO CONSTRUCT A FREQUENCY DISTRIBUTION

These are SAT Verbal (SATV) scores for a group of students who were selected to participate in a high school Language Arts enrichment program. The lowest SATV score is 320 and the highest is 699. The frequency distribution orders the 50 scores from lowest to highest and then tally marks are placed to show the frequency each score was obtained. Percentages (the relative frequencies) are calculated to provide even more information to you. Finally, cumulative frequencies and cumulative percentages are added to complete the picture. See Figure 2.2.

(N=50)

SATV Score	Tallies	Frequency (f)	Relative Frequency (%)	Cumulative Frequency	Cumulative Frequency (%)
320	///////	7	14%	7	14%
420	///////////////	15	30%	22	44%
430	//////	6	12%	28	56%
435	////	4	8%	32	64%
445	////	4	8%	36	72%
450	////	4	8%	40	80%
459	/	1	2%	41	82%
467	//////	6	12%	47	94%
479	/	1	2%	48	96%
689	/	1	2%	49	98%
699	/	1	2%	50	100%

Figure 2.2.   **Frequency Distribution of SAT Verbal Scores**

From this frequency distribution, you can draw some important conclusions:

- Most of the scores were low.
- The most frequently occurring score was 420.
- There is a broad range of scores from the highest (699) to the lowest (320) score.
- 96% got a score below 500.
- Two scores (699 and 689) were very different from other scores.
- More than half of the students scored 430 or below.

CLASS INTERVALS

Sometimes your data set is not as small (and manageable) as the SATV data set in terms of the number of student scores and the values of the student data. Let's say that you have twice as many in your sample of students—100 scores on the SAT Math.

You might want to use a shorthand called *class intervals*. The number of classifications of data (classes) can be reduced by combining several of the actual scores into an interval or band of scores. You are essentially consolidating the data into bundles to make it more manageable and comprehensible.

A good rule of thumb is to have between ten to twenty class intervals, altogether. This is particularly true if you intend to graph your frequency distribution data into a frequency polygon or histogram, which will be discussed shortly. Ten to 20 class intervals will summarize your data without distorting the shape of your graph. Too few intervals compress the data and thus conceal meaningful changes in the shape of your graph. Too many intervals stretch out the data and consequently they are not summarized enough for a clear visualization.

There are two general rules for using class intervals:

1. The class interval should be of such size that between ten and twenty intervals will cover the total range of scores. This provides for a manageable number of intervals without losing the general shape of the distribution of scores.

2. Whenever possible, the width of the class interval should be an odd rather than an even number. Under this rule, the midpoint of the interval will be a whole number rather than a fraction. This will become important when you graph your data.

HOW TO CONSTRUCT A FREQUENCY DISTRIBUTION USING CLASS INTERVALS

- First, determine the range in your frequency distribution from your highest score to your lowest. For the point of illustration, we have a low score of 320 and a high score of 767. The difference or *range* is (767 minus 320) 447.
- Divide the range by either 10 or 20 to get the number of intervals that makes the most sense and is most manageable. For 10, you would divide 447 by 10 and it would yield 45 as the class interval. For 20, you would divide 447 by 20 and get 22 as the class interval. For the sake of illustration we choose 10 so our class interval is 45.
- Begin your intervals a little below your lowest score; in our data it is 320. With 45-point increments, our first class interval is 300–344.
- Once you set up your class intervals, then you proceed the same way you did with the Frequency Distribution in Figure 2.2. Use tallies for the interval in which your student's score falls. A tally would note a score of 396 in the interval of 391–436.

Figure 2.3 displays what our Frequency Distribution with class intervals would look like.

(N=100)

Class Intervals Of 45	Tallies	Frequency (f)	Relative Frequency (%)	Cumulative frequency	Cumulative frequency (%)
300-344	/	1	1%	1	1%
345-390	/////	6	6%	7	7%
391-436	/////////////////////////	25	25%	32	32%
437-482	//////////////////	18	18%	50	50%
483-528	///////////	11	11%	61	61%
529-574	////////////	12	12%	73	73%
575-620	/////////	9	9%	82	82%
621-666	//////	6	6%	88	88%
667-712	//////	6	6%	94	94%
713-758	/////	5	5%	99	99%
759-800	/	1	1%	100	100%

Figure 2.3.   Frequency Distribution of SAT Math Scores with Class Intervals

As you can see, using class intervals to construct a frequency distribution makes it easy to analyze as well as to present your data. Again, important conclusions can be drawn:

- Most of the scores were low.
- The most frequently occurring scores were between 391 and 436.
- There is a broad range of scores from below 345 to over 758.
- 50% got a score below 483.
- There were a few extremely high and extremely low scores.

As a note, using class intervals is less cumbersome when your data are continuous and have a wide range of values. Think about the variable of *age* and the adults in your community if you were conducting a high school alumni survey. Listing all possible ages might begin at eighteen and go beyond 100 or more years! Doing a tally of each and every age would require a lot of paper—never mind time. This is a case when categorizing your variable into class intervals is a good idea. You might use intervals of five years in this case so those class intervals would look like this. There would be less than 20 intervals for adult ages.

Class Intervals for Age
18–22
23–27
28–32
33–37
38–42
43–47

48–52
53–57
58–62
63–67
68–72 and so forth.

On the other hand, there are times when using class intervals shortchanges the picture; you lose valuable data. Think about the variable "*years that teachers have been in the field of education.*" If you used class intervals, you would lose key information. A teacher who is brand new, one who has been with you for only one year, and one who has been on staff for two years may be very different from each other. If you collapsed the "years" in the field of education into intervals of five as shown above, you would lose important insights. Much of this is common sense. Deliberate what value the information has to you for data driven decisions. What is the information you want to uncover with your data?

WHY FREQUENCY DISTRIBUTIONS ARE HELPFUL

Whenever you compile a set of data, it is highly recommended that you first set up a frequency distribution and study it. Knowing your data thoroughly is critical before you begin to dig deeper into knowing what it means. Besides developing an expertise with your data set, there are several practical aspects to the development of frequency distributions.

- You can identify atypical or odd scores like that in Figure 2.2 (SATV 699 and SATV689). You have to be able to identify outlier scores before you can determine what you should do with them. It is important to decide whether to keep or discard outlier scores.
- You can compare the spread of the scores visually. If you set up two frequency distributions representing two of your third grade classrooms, and you see that their performance on math is different, this might impact your instructional strategies.
- By indicating the frequency that each value occurred in the distribution, this information could help you to make decisions about statistical analyses you will execute later on. This is particularly true with categorical variables. For example, if ethnic membership shows few students in one category, you may want to combine it with another that it is similar to so that statistical analyses can be executed.

• Finally, the frequency distribution may reveal data entry errors that you typed in accidentally. If you had a value of 099 on the SATM data, you would know that that was an incorrect entry. You would be able to make your correction and not run the data blindly, compromising the purity of your data set.

GRAPHING

The frequency distribution is an excellent tool for displaying data and inspecting your data. Yet, they do not convey the information as quickly or as impressively as graphs do. Graphing allows us to see the shape of a distribution. Graphs are designed to help the user obtain an intuitive feeling for the data at a glance. Their message should be readily apparent.

An effective graph is simple and clean. It should not attempt to present so much information that it is difficult to comprehend. It should be complete within itself and require little if any explanation in the narrative.

BENEFITS OF USING GRAPHS

Graphs are most beneficial to educators because they can provide a summary data sheet as well as an opportunity to eyeball your data. By looking at the *shape of the curve* (the hump) in your graph you can make some general conclusions quickly about the scores in your data set. The illustrations in Figure 2.4 will help in interpreting shapes.

• If the curve has a hump in the middle, its symmetry means that you have most scores in the middle of the range—few high and few low scores. (Figure 2.4 A).
• If the hump of the curve is inclined toward the left, you have more low scores in your data set. The tail of this type of curve indicates atypical or odd scores in your data. In this case, there was a minority of high scores. (positively skewed Figure 2.4 B).
• If the hump of the curve is to the right, you have more high scores in your data set. The tail of this type of curve indicates atypical or odd scores in your data. In this case, there was a minority of low scores. (negatively skewed Figure 2.4 C).
• If the hump of the curve is flat, you have scores that are spread out a great deal. Scores are all over the map. (platykurtic Figure 2.4 D).
• If the hump of the curve is peaked, your scores are very similar. There is not much difference among scores. (leptokurtic Figure 2.4 E).

A

Most scores are in the middle with few high and few low scores.
(Normal Curve)

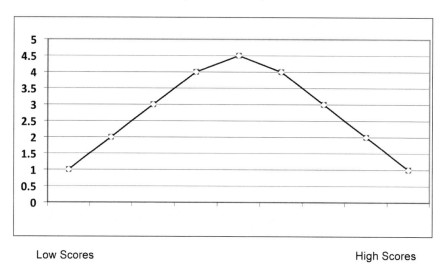

Low Scores   High Scores

B

Mostly low scores in frequency distribution and few high scores.
(Positively skewed)

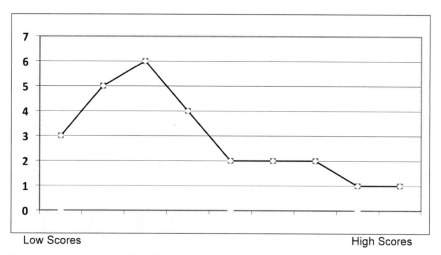

Low Scores   High Scores

Figure 2.4   Interpreting the Shapes of Curves in Frequency Polygons (A to E)

C

Mostly high scores in frequency distribution and few low scores.
(Negatively skewed)

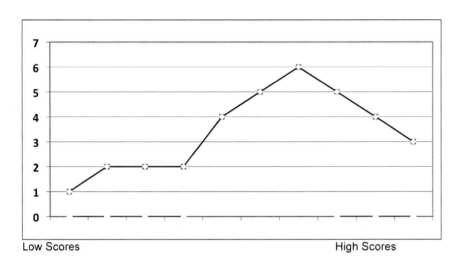

Low Scores   High Scores

D
Scores are spread out and there is no common performance.
(Platykurtic)

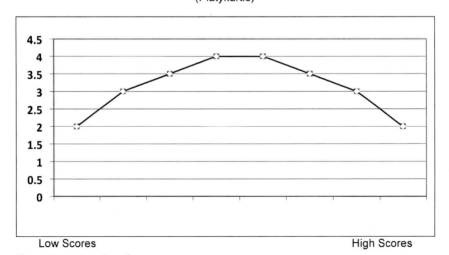

Low Scores   High Scores

Figure 2.4. (*continued*)

E

Scores are very similar with few differences among scores.
(Leptokurtic)

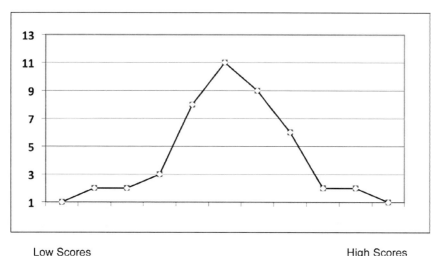

Low Scores   High Scores

Figure 2.4. (*continued*)

The discussion about shapes of graphs will have more meaning in subsequent chapters.

FREQUENCY POLYGONS

To construct a graph from a set of data, we start with the frequency distribution. A frequency distribution can be graphed into a *frequency polygon*. This is how you convert a frequency distribution into a frequency polygon.

Draw a vertical side or *ordinate* axis of your graph. This is called the *y*-axis. On the *y*-axis it is an accepted practice for the frequencies to be plotted. The horizontal axis, called the *abscissa,* is used to plot the variable that you are displaying data for. The horizontal axis is the *x*-axis. As a rule of thumb for good visual presentation, the vertical axis should be roughly two-thirds the length of the horizontal axis.

Connect the points or dots that intersect from the scores or score interval on the abscissa axis to the frequencies noted on the ordinate axis. If class intervals are used, connect the midpoint of the interval on the horizontal axis with the frequency on the vertical axis. This is why it is helpful to use odd numbers for the span of your class interval. The midpoint is easy to identify.

As a note, if the range in frequencies is large, you may want to start the vertical axis with a value that is not zero (0). When you do this, it is a good idea to use a jagged edge in the beginning of your vertical line so that it is clear that there is a break in the scale. With our SAT Math data we do not need this since we are starting at the low end of the SAT distribution of scores. The SAT range actually begins with the score of 200.

A frequency polygon for our SAT Math data with Class Intervals looks like that depicted in Figure 2.5.

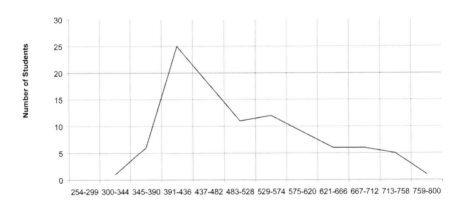

SAT Math Class Intervals

Figure 2.5. Frequency Polygon

Plotting the data this way allows the graph to take on a shape. When you look at that shape, you can make a conclusion about the data from the frequency distribution. When there are a lot of data from many subjects, the frequency polygon looks like a smooth curve. When there are fewer values, it is jagged. Either way, the picture tells a story. This is a picture that gives us an immediate message about our data. We look at it and can infer something about our data. For our SAT Math graph, the simple message is that there are many low scores in this distribution.

We can also construct a cumulative frequency polygon from our frequency distribution if we have included cumulative data. We can either use the cumulative frequencies or we can use the percentages on the vertical axis, where 100% is the highest and 0% is the lowest value. Cumulative

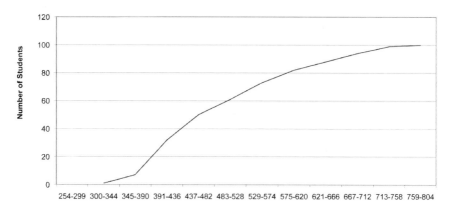

SAT Math Class Intervals

Figure 2.6. Cumulative Frequency Polygon

frequency polygons are known as *ogives*. Please refer to Figure 2.6 for an illustration of a *Cumulative* Frequency Polygon on the SAT Math data with Class Intervals.

HISTOGRAMS, BAR CHARTS, AND PICTOGRAPHS

A *histogram* is another pictorial representation of a frequency distribution table. The vertical scale should begin at zero (0). Again, use the jagged edge if you cannot begin it with zero (0). A general rule in laying out the histogram is to make the height of the vertical scale equal to approximately two-thirds the length of the horizontal scale. Otherwise, the histogram may appear to be out of proportion.

A vertical bar is constructed above each class interval equal in height to its frequency. All of the rectangles have equal width. This is a very common way to display data. You can also set up a cumulative frequency histogram, as we did with cumulative frequency polygons. We can use the cumulative frequencies or we can use the percentages on the vertical axis, where 100% is the highest and 0% is the lowest value. Figure 2.7 displays what a histogram would look like for our SAT data with Class Intervals.

A *bar graph* is a convenient graphing device that is particularly useful for displaying nominal data such as gender and ethnicity. The various categories are located along the horizontal axis. The frequency, as always, is on the vertical axis. The height of each bar is equal to the frequency for that category. This is a helpful tool to see differences in your data for individual groups on some variable.

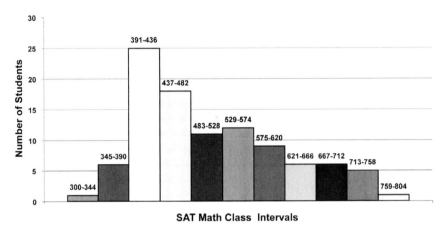

Figure 2.7. Histogram

One difference between a histogram and a bar graph is that with the histogram the bars are placed next to each other to show when one interval begins and the other one ends. The data are continuous, and interval/ratio scaled. However, because the data are *nominal* in bar graphs, we do not connect the bars, preventing any implication of continuity. We separate the bars and use equal space to separate one bar from the next. Drawing the bars in a bar graph creates ease in interpretation. A bar graph is displayed in Figure 2.8 of middle schools and their respective disciplinary referral rates.

A pictograph uses pictures or symbols in place of numbers. Figure 2.9 portrays a pictograph of the number of books read by a fourth grade class during the school week. It uses a book icon, representing five books read for each day Monday through Friday.

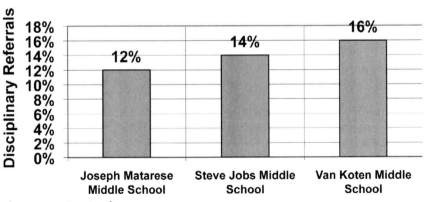

Figure 2.8. Bar Graph

Days of Week						
Monday	📖					
Tuesday	📖	📖				
Wednesday	📖	📖				
Thursday	📖	📖				
Friday	📖	📖	📖	📖	📖	📖

📖 **= 5 books read by 4th Grade class**

Figure 2.9. Pictograph

PIE CHARTS

Another method to display categorical data is by using a *pie chart* which is easy and user-friendly. You can show categories of a variable by dividing up "the pie." Use 100% of the area in the circle and divide it up proportionally to your categories of interest. Figure 2.10 displays a pie chart that reflects a secondary school faculty and the types of degrees they hold.

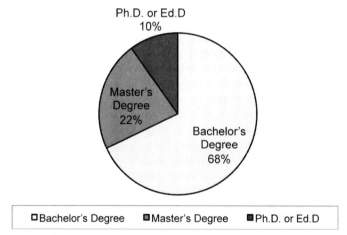

Figure 2.10. Pie Chart

CONSTRUCTING YOUR GRAPHS

Graphing is an excellent way to present your data to the untrained eye. There are two recommendations to observe when constructing your graphs.

1. A graph is a picture. The message should be readily apparent. Keeping it simple is a good practice to follow when graphing or even when constructing your tables. Those who will be viewing the graph or reading your reports are not as involved in your data and analysis as you are and have other thoughts competing for their attention. Don't waste their time with graphs that are either too simplistic or overly complex. Use them judiciously and with deliberation.

2. Avoid the temptation to emphasize your point or position by "adjusting" the vertical axis. This creates a *truncated* graph. The vertical scale is cut off or restricted so that the information becomes distorted and the picture misleading. This is a practice that the media often use in reporting or sensationalizing stories for the public (untrained) eye. The axes are exaggerated so that the graph presents dramatic results that were rather "ho hum." The vertical axis is restricted to a short range, causing overemphasis of

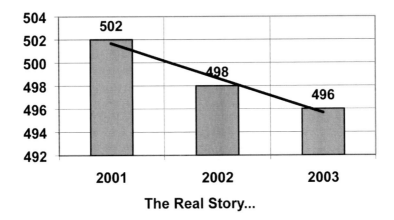

The Real Story...

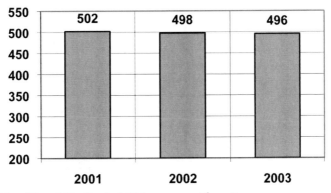

Figure 2.11. "Steep" Decline in SAT Scores over Three Years

the results in either a positive or negative light. The graph in Figure 2.11 reports a "steep decline in SAT scores." But look how the vertical scale has been adjusted to begin at 492, distorting the picture. The drop over a three-year period is negligible—from 502 to 496! An initial glance at the graph would cause your secondary school principal to faint—before he or she could find out the real story in the actual data.

CHAPTER SUMMARY

The process of becoming an expert with your data is work. Setting up the frequency distribution for your data set, graphing it, and then interpreting what it conveys are often-skipped steps in data management. The time it takes to do the "grunt" work as a preliminary step is a meaningful investment of time. There are advantages to be gained in many areas. You will be able to reduce errors, make wise decisions about statistical techniques, and ultimately provide a better foundation for your decisions. This has implications that are far-reaching. Take the time to know your data set. The value will be well worth the hours spent.

Chapter Three

Presenting a Mountain of Data with One Number

The importance of getting to know your data was presented in chapter 2. The frequency distributions and the graphing techniques help to produce a basic profile of your data set. Taking the time to construct them helps to indicate the characteristics of your data.

There are also certain statistics that are generated for the purpose of describing the distributions of your data or the relationships between your variables. They are called *descriptive statistics.* These very useful statistics bring together large amounts of data so they can be presented and comprehended with minimal effort.

Descriptive statistics are widely applied. A good example of a real life application is the U.S. Census. By using some of the popular descriptive statistics, we get a sense of important characteristics of households in the United States. For example, descriptive statistics that are available in Census data may indicate:

- Average household size
- Ethnic and gender breakdowns
- Employment rates
- Number of households in poverty
- Characteristics of homeowners and renters
- Percent of children in different age categories
- Per capita income
- Levels of educational attainment

Schools can do the same thing with important variables such as class sizes, standards-based test scores, school attendance, primary language spoken in the home, college placement, and dropout rates to name just a few. If we had to generate this type of information from looking at raw data, it would be too complex to grasp and readily understood. Descriptive statistics make it easy to get a sense of what is typical or average.

Measures of *central tendency* represent an important collection of descriptive statistics. These are designed to describe the *central part* of the distribution that you created with your frequency distribution. They tell where most scores appear to group, cluster, or fall together—their commonality. In other words, they tell us the average. With one single number you can obtain an accurate picture of your entire distribution. It suggests the typical performance of a group as a whole and is a concise description.

There are three measures of central tendency—the mean, the median, and the mode.

THE MEAN (X BAR)

The *mean* represents a whole data set with one single number! The mean is the arithmetic average value in your distribution of scores. To obtain the mean you add up all of the scores (Xs) and divide by the total number of scores (*n*) in your distribution. As a rule, your data set of scores should tend to cluster together and not be spread all over. The beauty of the mean is that you utilize each score in your distribution to calculate it. As a result, it is the most stable measure of central tendency and the one used most often. Since it is an average, you probably have been calculating a mean often in your everyday life. In professional journals, the mean is often noted as "*M.*"

Here is a simple example to illustrate the use of the mean. During this past school year, the Board of Education was contemplating the creation of additional elementary school classroom space. The three neighborhood elementary schools were brimming with children. This was due to recent in-migrations, where families were moving from cities to a more rural location. So the Board members decided to find out what the average class size was in order to arm themselves with supporting data for overcrowding and ultimately for additional classroom space.

Although class sizes were compiled for all grade levels, the data set for te10n third grade classrooms was reported as follows (Figure 3.1).

The mean was calculated as 30 students per classroom—larger than what was desirable. Here was the evidence the Board of Education needed. With just one number representing all 10 schools the Board had a solid piece of information for data driven decisions.

Third Grade Classrooms	Class Size
Class 1	28
Class 2	28
Class 3	29
Class 4	29
Class 5	29
Class 6	31
Class 7	31
Class 8	32
Class 9	32
Class 10	33
Mean	**30**

Figure 3.1.　Class Size Data for Third Grade Classrooms

The mean is a very good measure of central tendency.

- It is based on more precise measurement scales such as interval and ratio. Sometimes ordinal is used, too. This may occur with rating scales, performance scales, or satisfaction scales where averages are useful. Purists would object to the use of a mean with ordinal data simply because the units of measurement are not exact. However, in many educational applications, ordinal data is used with the mean because it makes sense. That is the determinant of when to apply the mean to your data if it is ordinal scaled. If it makes sense in producing good information for strategic decisions, by all means use it. Certainly, no mean can be calculated with nominal scaled variables.
- As mentioned before, *all* the scores in a data set are used to calculate the mean. This is another advantage.
- Finally, many of the powerful statistical analyses rely on the mean to calculate formulas for statistical significance. So the mean has become the Queen of Central Tendency. But this royal designation should be avoided if your data set possesses *outliers*.

OUTLIERS

An *outlier* is an extremely high or low score in your distribution. It is an *atypical* score and does not resemble most of the other scores in your distribution. It affects the calculation of the mean and makes the mean less representative of the group. While the mean is looking to create typical performance in your data set, the outlier is atypical. If you recall, we had two outliers in the SAT Math data set in chapter 2.

What happens is that outliers cause the mean to shift in the direction of the outlier. If the outlier is a high score, the mean is calculated higher than it should be. If it is a low score, the mean is lower than it should be to represent the whole group. Outliers cause your distribution to become skewed. This problem is particularly true if the number of scores in your distribution is small.

You can tell if you have outliers in your data set by setting up a frequency distribution and then graphing a frequency polygon. This is another advantage of taking the time to produce frequency distributions and using the graphing techniques. If you have an asymmetrical curve, outliers are hanging around. The SAT frequency polygons and histograms in chapter 2 suffered from the existence of outliers in the data set. The curves in the graphs were irregular as opposed to being balanced in form.

Going back to the example of classroom size, let's alter the data set with two particularly small third grade classrooms. The data set would look like that in Figure 3.2.

Third Grades Classrooms	Class Size
Class 1	28
Class 2	28
Class 3	29
Class 4	29
Class 5	29
Class 6	31
Class 7	31
Class 8	32
Class 9 outlier	11
Class 10 outlier	12
Mean	**26**

Figure 3.2.   Class Size Data for Third Grade Classrooms with Outliers

Here, the outlier caused the mean to shift down to 26 children per classroom. The presence of the outlier decreased the case for additional classroom space; but it is not a good representation of average class size in your school system. Most class sizes in your data set distribution are around 29 to 30. If you used the mean as the measure of central tendency in this case, you would be presenting an underestimated picture of need.

What should you do? Examine your data through the grunt work of developing a frequency distribution, and then use *more than one measure* of central tendency. One of the best, when your data has outliers, is the *median*.

THE MEDIAN

When there are extreme scores or outliers in your distribution, the *median* is the preferred measure of central tendency. The median is the counting average. It is simply the midpoint in your distribution of ranked, ordered scores. The median can be used with ordinal, interval, and ratio scaled data. Nominal data are inappropriate.

To calculate the median, list all of the values in your distribution from the lowest to the highest and then find the *midpoint*—the place where it divides your distribution into equal halves. That is, 50% of all scores is above and 50% is below (Table 3.1).

The Median—Odd Number of Scores in Your Distribution

If there is an *odd* number of scores in your distribution, the median is easy to identify. Find the midpoint in the range of high to low scores. That midpoint is the median, since half of the scores are above it and half are below it. A formula can be used to locate the position in an ordered set of data.

[Median = Number of scores plus 1 divided by 2]

If you had 11 scores (an odd number), the formula would be $(11 + 1)$, by 2 = 6. The median would be the sixth score in the set of data where the scores are listed in order from lowest to highest.

Here is an example where we have an odd number (11) of scores. The midpoint is the sixth score or the exact middle of the distribution. In this distribution, the median is 29, and 29 is an actual score in the data set.

Table 3.1.   The Median with Odd Number of Scores

Order of Scores Lowest to Highest	1st Score	2nd Score	3rd Score	4th Score	5th Score	6th Score	7th Score	8th Score	9th Score	10th Score	11th Score
The 11 Scores	28	28	29	29	29	29	31	31	32	32	33
					50%	Mid-point	50%				

The Median—Even Number of Scores in Your Distribution

If you have an even number of scores, find the two that make the centermost point, and then average them. If you have an even number of scores, the median may or may not be an actual score, depending on what the two midpoints are. If the midpoints are identical scores, then this is the median. If they need to be averaged, then the median will be an average and not an actual score in your distribution. That is why we say the median is the midpoint, a point not a score.

Here is an example of when this is true. In Figure 3.2, we had our class size data with the outliers in the group. Two classrooms had 11 and 12 children each. This outlier shifted our mean down to 26. So we decide to calculate a median.

The data set consisted of 10 scores altogether—an even number of scores. So we have to find the two midpoints and average them. The 10 scores are divided in half—with five scores on the left and five scores on the right. The median is calculated by taking two scores at the midpoint or center, and calculating a mean. In this case, there is a score of 29 on the left and a score of 31 on the right (Table 3.2).

The formula becomes [Center point 1 plus Center point 2] / 2 = Median

In this example, the application of the formula is $[29+31] = 60 / 2 = 30$ (the Median).

The median and midpoint of the distribution is 30. However, note that the median is not an actual score in the set of data. As you can see, the median is not affected one bit by the outliers of 11 and 12. While the mean was a 26, the median of 30 is much more representative of the data set. This is the greatest benefit of using the median. Oddball scores in the data set do not affect it. Although the median is not calculated by using all of the scores in

Table 3.2. The Median with an Even Number of Scores

Order of Scores Lowest to Highest	1st Score	2nd Score	3rd Score	4th Score	5th Score	6th Score	7th Score	8th Score	9th Score	10th Score
The 10 Scores	28	28	29	29	29	31	31	32	44	45

Center points

the distribution, as the mean is, the median plays an important role in stating the central tendency of your data set—especially if there are outlier scores.

THE MODE

The *mode* is an unsophisticated measure of central tendency. It is the most frequently occurring value in your distribution. It is a simple but rough statistic to calculate the central tendency of your data. The mode does not need to be calculated. If you look at your frequency distribution, a simple eyeball inspection of your data can tell you which score occurred most often. Look at the tallies or frequencies. It is quick and can be obtained with a glance. We did that in chapter 2 with our first data set of SAT Verbal scores. We looked at the frequency distribution in Figure 2.2 and could see that the mode was 420.

The mode provides little information beyond simply identifying the score in your data set that appears with the greatest frequency. Therefore, it should only be used when you have a large data set of scores, and not just a few. A small set of scores would not have enough frequency of occurrence built into it to develop a mode. You need many scores so that you can be certain which score turned up most often.

For example, in Figure 3.1 our class sizes contribute to a frequency distribution that looks like this. The mode is 29. It occurred the most often and in this case approximately three times. When there is *one* score that occurs with the most frequently in a distribution, we say the distribution is *unimodal* or when graphed, it has one hump due to the fact that there is one mode.

Many frequency distributions have more than one mode (Table 3.3). That is, more than one score turns up at the same high level of frequency. Two modes in a frequency distribution create a *bimodal* frequency distribution. This might occur in a set of data where two groups are very different on the variable measured. If graphed, there would be two humps in the curve or shape. For example, if "literacy" of preschoolers was the variable measured,

Table 3.3.   Frequency Distribution

Class Size	Frequency
28	2
29	3
31	2
32	2
33	1

two modes might indicate that differential literacy levels were attained in your preschool population. In Figure 3.3, there are two modes: 10 and 50. This could mean that those who achieved a 10 were not school-ready, and those who got 50 were school-ready. This has instructional implications for the Kindergarten teachers.

If there are more than two modes, the distribution is called *multimodal* and the graphing shows several humps or curves.

Preschool Literacy Scores	Tallies	Frequency (f)	
10	/////////	8	**MODE**
20		0	
30	/	1	
40	/	1	
50	////////	8	**MODE**
60	//	2	
70	///	3	
80	//	2	
90	//	2	

Figure 3.3.   A Bimodal Distribution with Two Modes

CHAPTER SUMMARY

Each measure of central tendency has a role to play in descriptive statistics. The mean is the preferred method of calculating the center of your data set. But when outliers emerge, the median is an alternative that is not affected by these unrepresentative scores. If you are in a hurry and want to get a ballpark feeling for the average, the mode will work with a quick glance at the frequency distribution table. Here is a summary of the three measures and when to use which one. The best advice is to report all three with an understanding of central tendency and how each is derived.

The mean

- If you want the greatest reliability
- If you will be calculating variability and other statistical computations
- If your distribution has no outliers
- If your data are interval, ratio, and ordinal scaled

The median

- If your distribution is skewed by outliers
- If your data are interval, ratio, or ordinal scaled

The mode

- If you need a quick estimate
- If you have nominal, ordinal, interval, or ratio scaled data
- If you can eyeball the data from a frequency distribution

Chapter Four

Understanding Why the Range in Your Data Is Important

So far, a case has been made about the importance of constructing a frequency distribution and plotting the data into a graph for a snapshot. Similarly, the value of the three measures of central tendency was established. They can indicate to us with a single number the general character of our set of data.

There is another essential step—measuring the *variability* of your data set. Many times, statistics are reported without mention of the variance or spread of scores. The media often report assessment data with only the mean as a statistic. This can create a misrepresentation of your data. This is why.

The variance is the manner in which your data are spread in either direction from the center of your distribution. It is important to know whether the scores tend to be homogeneous or whether they vary from each other. The measures of variability tell us how representative our mean is. Are the scores the same or are they spread out?

For example, look at the two sets of data for reading achievement in fourth grade (Table 4.1). The mean in both cases is 100. Given that statistic, both fourth grade classes seem to be progressing in the same fashion. Closer inspection of the data shows that, while Ms. Fondaire's class performed very much the same, Mr. Colon's class had some very high and very low scores. For Ms. Fondaire's class, the lowest score was 98 and the highest was 102. For Mr. Colon's class, the lowest score was 79 while the highest was 140. The spread or dispersion was great in Mr. Colon's class, where there was high variability. Conversely, the low variability in Ms. Fondaire's class was evident from the similar scores. There are practical implications for Mr. Colon that would be overlooked if just the mean were used to profile his classroom data.

Table 4.1.

Ms. Fondaire's Fourth Grade	Mr. Colon's Fourth Grade
98	140
102	80
99	79
100	100
99	100
100	79
102	80
98	140
Mean = 100	Mean = 100

There are several descriptive statistics that measure variability. The range, the variance, and the standard deviation, which are used quite often in educational settings, will be discussed next.

THE RANGE

The *range* is a very simple statistic and the most unsophisticated measure of variability. In this regard, it possesses characteristics analogous to the mode in central tendency. It is a rough estimate, quickly computed, but not tremendously stable. This is because it is computed with only two scores: the highest score and the lowest score in your distribution of scores. You subtract one from the other. The range for Ms. Fondaire's class would be 4 (102 minus 98) while the range for Mr. Colon's class would be 61 (140 minus 79)! Even this crude measure of variability is very helpful in providing us with information.

The range is influenced by the size of your data set. The larger the data set, the greater the likelihood of extreme values because you have more potential for outliers. This is a limitation of the range; outliers affect it. Since you are using only two scores in your data set to calculate the range, if there is an outlier at either end, it will influence the calculation.

VARIABILITY AND GRAPHS

Graphs, discussed in chapter 2, are quite useful in initially determining the variability in your distribution. The *shape* of the frequency polygons and histograms that are constructed from the frequency distribution can tell us the story about the spread of scores at a glance. This is another asset of the frequency distribution (and their respective graphs), and a further reason to use them in getting to know your data set.

If the hump or curve in your graph is markedly flat, the scores are spread out; there is a great deal of variability. This type of curve is called *platykurtic* and it means that your scores are spread out around the mean score of the distribution. On the other hand, if the hump or curve in your graph is peaked and tight, there is little spread in scores; the variability is low. This type of curve is called *leptokurtic* and it means that your scores are very close to the mean score of the distribution. (Please refer to Graphs D and E in Figure 2.4.)

Here are two graphs (Figures 4.1 and 4.2) that display the Numbers Theory scores for sixth grade students. The Intervention Group participated in a special math program and the Comparison Group did not. For both the mean score on the Open Response test was 6. As you can see, the students in the Intervention Group performed similarly, while Comparison Group scores were varied. In fact, the range was 10 (11 minus 1) for the Comparison Group and only 4 (8 minus 4) for the Intervention Group.

The shape of the curves immediately indicate the dispersion or spread of scores. For the Comparison Group the shape of the curve is flat (*platykurtic*). The message from the graph is that scores are spread out around the mean.

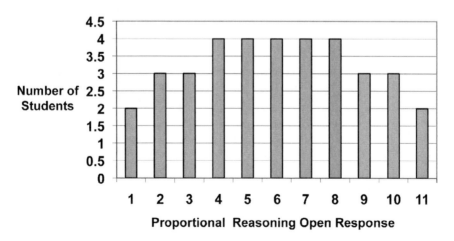

Figure 4.1. Comparison Group

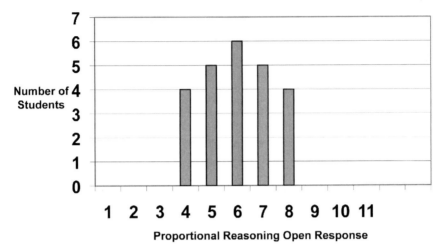

Figure 4.2.   Intervention Group

To claim that most students were performing as well without the enrichment program is false. For the Intervention Group the shape of the curve is
peaked (*leptokurtic*). The mean is an excellent measure of central tendency
because there is little spread. It would be safe to conclude that most Intervention Group students are performing better than the Comparison Group even
though mean scores are the same. If a statistical procedure were applied to
these data, there likely would be a significant difference between the Intervention and Comparison groups.

VARIANCE AND STANDARD DEVIATION

There are two additional measures of variability—the *variance* and the *standard deviation*. Both are much better indicators of dispersion in your data set
than the range is. This is because they use all of the scores in the data set in
their calculation (just as the mean does). While the mode and the range have
similar traits (quick, unsophisticated), the mean and the variance/standard
deviation are very much alike (precise, reliable). They are the kings of variability as the mean is the queen of central tendency. In addition, each of these
statistics relies on more precise measurement scales such as interval and ratio.
(Some educators use the ordinal scale but there is a trade-off in precision.)

The formulas for calculating both the variance and the standard deviation
can be found in any math or statistics book. However, if you are using a
statistical software package, these will be calculated for you. Conceptually,
each of these statistics is based upon how much each score in your data set

deviates from the mean, and then putting the deviation scores into a formula for computation. The variance is the standard deviation squared, and the standard deviation is the square root of the variance. So they are more or less "siblings" in the realm of variance. The symbol for reporting the variance is "sigma squared" (s^2). The symbol for standard deviation is SD or sigma (s). These symbols are what you might see in professional journals.

Because both the variance and standard deviation are calculated by deviations from the mean in your data set, their value is tremendous. With one single number, you can tell whether most of the scores in your data set cluster closely around the mean, or are spread out. The larger the standard deviation, the more spread out are your scores in your data set.

For example, let's consider the SAT. Last year our juniors took the SAT Verbal and got a mean of 600 and an SD of 50. This year our juniors took the SAT Verbal and got a mean score of 610 and SD of 120. The newspapers report a 10-point gain in our SAT Verbal performance. Our scores rose from 600 to 610. What appears to be good news for our school system is in fact a hidden problem. The standard deviation of 120 shows outlier scores have shifted the mean upward and artificially created the image that all of our scores were rising. While we can celebrate in this good news this year, it puts a strain on next year when we have to explain to the public why the scores are back down to 600. If the standard deviation were calculated in addition to the mean, there would be a more accurate presentation of our junior students' performance.

This scenario is typically what happens often in the reporting of standardized testing results. What is *not* reported is the standard deviation. This leaves schools vulnerable to public assessments based on a few points—up or down—in mean score performance. If school systems used both the mean and the SD, they would not be vulnerable when there are a few point gains and losses. In this particular example, last year's juniors performed better on the SAT Verbal. The SD was smaller (50) and thus the mean score of 600 was better able to represent overall performance. This year, we had a large SD of 120. This means that although the mean was higher, it did not represent our juniors' performance as well. There was a spread of SAT Verbal scores around the mean.

Here is a sound policy in educational settings. *Whenever you report the mean, you should report the standard deviation.* They are the statistical couple. The standard deviation tells you a great deal—how representative your mean is as a measure of central tendency for your data set.

Look at the data for the *number of suspensions* from the three middle schools in your district (Table 4.2). At face value three middle schools in

Table 4.2.

Suspensions in Three Middle Schools	Mean Per Month	Standard Deviation
Peak Middle School	60	2
Dressel Middle School	60	1
Hayes Middle School	60	15

your district have the exact same number of suspensions per month—60. So, you assume that this is typical or average. However, the standard deviations tell a very different story. For Peak Middle School and Dressel Middle School the means are very representative of the monthly average for suspensions. The SD is small for both. If you actually drew a frequency polygon from the frequency distribution data per month, these two schools would have leptokurtic curves. The values would be close to the mean.

But this is not true for Hayes Middle School. This school has a greater spread of scores around its mean of 60, as signified by the standard deviation of 15. The frequency polygon for the Hayes Middle School data would be flat. And actually, the median might be the better measure of central tendency in this case. At the very least, it would behoove smart administrators to examine both the mean and median before they designed a behavioral intervention on average suspensions per month.

NORMAL CURVES OR NORMAL DISTRIBUTIONS

The standard deviation is one of the most valuable tools that educators have at their disposal. One of its primary uses is in helping us to interpret test score performance. To fully understand its value, a discussion of *the normal curve* is necessary. (Some of the information about the normal curve should be memorized; that is how fundamental it is.)

Most of the data that we use in education is thought to be *normally distributed.* This means that if we constructed a frequency distribution and then graphed a frequency polygon, the hump or curve would be symmetrical. When a graphed, the frequency distribution resembles a bell; it means that there are a few scores on either end of the hump or curve; most scores are in the middle.

AREA UNDER THE NORMAL CURVE

A normal distribution creates *a bell-shaped* curve or frequency polygon. These are some characteristics of the normal curve:

1. It has one mode (unimodal).
2. The mean, median, and mode are exactly the same number.
3. It is symmetrical and bell-shaped.
4. The two tails (ends of the curve) do not touch the abscissa (*x*-axis).

When you draw a normal curve (Figure 4.3), you observe these four characteristics. Because the mean, median, and mode are dead center, and the curve is symmetrical, the normal curve, drawn in most statistics books, has ordinates or vertical lines from the top of the curve to the baseline. When you look at the picture of a normal curve, visualize thousands of children standing under the curve; imagine faces looking at you. This is what the normal curve is representing—data of individuals on whatever variables you are examining. Let's visualize a state mandated performance test and where loads of students are standing underneath the curve.

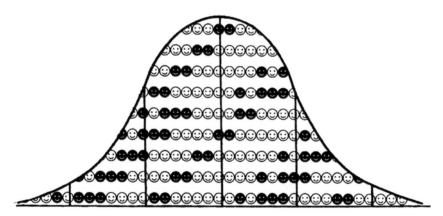

Figure 4.3. What the Normal Curve Represents: People

As you can see, most of our students are standing in the center, creating the huge hump. This is where the mean is. That makes sense since the mean reports the central tendency of the students' scores. Then, you can see that as we move away from the center or mean, the number of kids standing underneath the outer areas of the curve is fewer and fewer until we get to the tails of the curves and there are a couple of outliers standing around.

                               Chapter Four

This is a typical pattern of data. Most people attain very similar scores and thus they fall close to the middle—the mean. Fewer perform dissimilar to their group.

THE TYPICAL GRAPH OF THE NORMAL CURVE

In Figure 4.4, the vertical lines are drawn from the top of the curve to the baseline at zero (0) and at numbers 1, 2, and 3 *to the left and to the right of zero.* Zero (0) represents the mean score or dead center. These vertical lines mark off areas under the curve and represent standard deviation units (1, 2, and 3) or distance from the mean. The standard deviation units act like a ruler and divide up the area under the normal curve.

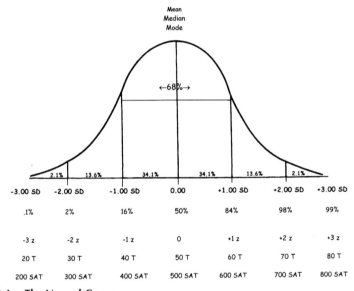

Figure 4.4. The Normal Curve

The base of the normal curve is divided into six units with 3 SD above and 3 SD below the mean. Entries within the graph indicate the proportion of the total area (or number of scores) that falls into each of the six segments or demarcations. These are the proportions of area under the SD cut-offs.

- between the mean (0) and +1 SD units are 34.1% of all scores;
- between the mean (0) and −1 SD units are 34.1% of all scores;
- between ±1SD are 68% of all scores;
- between +1 SD and +2 SD units are 13.6% of all scores;
- between −1 SD and −2 SD units are 13.6% of all scores;

- between ±2 SD are 95% of all scores;
- between + 2 SD and +3 SD units are 2.1% of all scores;
- between –2 SD and −3 SD units are 2.1% of all scores;
- between ±3SD are 99% of all scores.

Since we know that the mean is dead center, it is at the fiftieth percentile mark. The next bit of information is important to educators in interpreting scores.

- *One standard deviation above the mean* is an area of 34%. This indicates that if your score is 1 SD above the mean, you performed better than 84% of all other scores in the distribution (50% plus 34%).
- *One standard deviation below the mean* is an area of 34%. This indicates that if your score is 1 SD below the mean, you performed better than only 16% (50% minus 34%).
- *One standard deviation above and below the mean* is an area of 68%.
- Over two-thirds of the students perform within one standard deviation of the mean (±1SD). If you look at the normal curve and pretend again that students are standing underneath it, then this is very logical. It is the area where *most scores fall*, creating the large hump.
- *Two standard deviations above the mean* cover an area of 48%. Between the center (0) and +1 SD there is 34% of the area under the curve. Between +1 SD and +2 SD there is 14% of the area under the curve. As you can see, the further you get from the center, the less area there is under the curve. This is because most scores/values are in the center where the hump is. Again, think of people standing underneath the curve.

If a student in your school gets a score that is two standard deviations above the mean, he or she is in a select few. They have performed better than 98% of all students (50% plus 48%).

- *Two standard deviations below the mean* cover an area of 48%. Between the center and −1 SD there is 34% of the area under the curve. Between −1 SD and −2 SD there is 14% of the area under the curve. If a student in your school gets a score that is two standard deviations below the mean, he or she is in the minority. They have performed better than only 2% of all students (50% minus 48%).
- *Two standard deviations above and below the mean* is an area of 95%. If you look at the normal curve and pretend again that students are standing underneath it to create the hump in it, then the percentage of 95% is very logical. Almost all of the students perform within two standard deviation units of the mean (±2 SD).

The standard deviation units, together with the percentage of area under the normal curve, can be used to determine the relative position of scores above and below the mean. The information is defined as the "distance from the mean." This is extremely useful to educators.

All standardized tests have means and standard deviations reported. So educators can compare their entire school system or even an individual student's performance to the national norms. If there is a statewide test, you can be sure that mean and standard deviations by key segments exist for your comparisons. Or, you can calculate your overall district's mean and standard deviations, and then compare individual schools to these baselines. Finally, you can calculate a mean and standard deviation for one segment of students and then compare individual student test scores to these.

The normal curve gives educators the ability to make a call on where their school system, schools, or even individual students stand in relation to all others. This is because the percentiles under the normal curve indicate the relative position of those falling above and below a certain designation.

Here is a model (Figure 4.5) that you can follow to set up a chart for any of your data sets. Substitute your own mean and your own standard deviation at each SD unit. Then use the areas under the normal curve to pinpoint the performance levels you are trying to discern.

Calculations	-3SD	–2SD	–1SD	0	+1SD	+2SD	+3SD
from test →	(Mean-3SD)	(Mean-2SD)	(Mean-1SD	(Mean)	(Mean+1SD)	(Mean+2SD)	(Mean+3SD)

Figure 4.5.

An easy to comprehend example are SAT scores. The vertical axis from the top of the normal curve to the mean divides the curve in half. This means that 50% of all test takers get around 500 as a score. We can infer that if they get a score of 400, they are one SD unit below the mean and performing similar to 16% of their peers. If they get 600, they are 1 SD unit above the mean and performing better than 84% of their peers. If they get a 700, they are in the advantaged minority. They are scoring two SD units above their peers and performing better than 98% of those taking the test. Conversely, a score of 300 means that they did better than only 2% of their peers. This is a great deal of information that you can obtain when you know the mean and standard deviation unit of any data set of scores—not just standardized tests.

As a caution, educators would be wise to calculate their own local norms on standardized tests. This would give more reliable and valid data for your particular school system, and not subject you to the misrepresentation of performance in the media. Sometimes, a gain of 2 or 3 points is viewed as a success, while a decline of 2 or 3 points is reported as a failure for local schools. This is a tremendous disservice, but few schools systems are armed with the correct data to present a truer picture. You can do this retrospectively, too, since the data are in your records from past years. It is a matter of calculating means and standard deviations—time well invested.

A PRACTICAL EXAMPLE

Here is an example that demonstrates the practical utility of collecting this type of strategic information. Let's say that you decide to calculate the Mean and SD for your junior year students taking the SAT from the year 2012. Here is what you see.

Table 4.3.

Year	Mean	SD	±1 SD (68% of scores)
2012	500	20	480–520
2013	500	60	440–560
2014	490	20	470–510

At first glance it looks as if your juniors took a dive in their SAT performance in the year 2014. They dropped from 500 in 2013 to 490 in 2014. This is a ten-point drop that the media might report as a failure. However, you look at the standard deviations and note that a larger standard deviation unit (SD = 60) was obtained in 2013. This signifies that your 2013 juniors performed more heterogeneously than in previous years. Scores varied more around the mean. Conversely, the 2014 scores were very similar to those in 2012—when you consider the SD. The 68% or hump under the curve was more alike in 2012 and 2014 than in 2013 even though the mean score dropped down.

If educators want to strengthen their data further, they would profile *demographics* on students who are taking tests from year to year. They should be asking the following question: Has the demographic composition of the student population changed? For the hypothetical data above, it may be likely that in-migration has brought more diversity to your school district in the year 2013. The diverse populations could account for the variability in scores. However, if you do not know the baseline information on both performance and your local demographics you cannot fully address the headline in your local newspaper that charges "School is doing a poor job preparing students for college: SAT drops 10 points."

STANDARD SCORES OR z SCORES

A *standard* or *z score* is another useful tool to educators. Its symbol is lowercase z. Standard scores describe a particular score's position in a distribution by expressing the score's distance above or below the mean. For example, if you knew a student's score on a standardized test, you could tell exactly where under the normal curve this student would be "standing." Then you could infer the level of that student's performance.

Here is how z scores work. You have a score on any given measure. As mentioned before, the symbol for a score is X. You calculate a z score by subtracting your score (X) from the mean and then dividing it by the standard deviation (SD). This is your z score. If the z score is negative, then your standard score or z score is below the mean. If it is positive, it is above the mean. If it is zero, it is the mean.

The beauty of the z score is that you are able to find out exactly where under the normal curve you are. Most statistics books have a table that converts area under the normal curve from the mean ordinate to the z scores. A portion is displayed in Figure 4.6. Here is how it is used.

Let's say that you achieved a z score of 1.34. You look in the Table for Percent of Total Area under the Normal Curve. The intersection of 1.3 (vertical) and the .04 (horizontal) equal the z score of 1.34. The number at the intersection is 40.9. (This is highlighted so that you can see how it was located in the table.) This would make sense since we know that 1 SD is 34% and we have a z score that is *over* 1 SD. This is great information but made even better since we know that zero (0) is 50% in the normal curve. So we add the 40.9% from our z score with the 50% to create a percentage of 90.9%. We can conclude that our performance was 90.9% better than everyone else was who took the test.

SKEWED DISTRIBUTIONS

Before closing this chapter, we need to address the fact that oftentimes our distributions or data sets are not normally distributed. When we use the statistics that will be discussed in the following chapters, there is an assumption that our data sets will be normally distributed. Many times they are; but some-

z	.00	.01	.02	.03	.04	.05	.06	.07	.08	.09
0.0	.0000	.0040	.0080	.0120	.0160	.0199	.0239	.0279	.0319	.0359
0.1	.0398	.0438	.0478	.0517	.0557	.0596	.0636	.0675	.0714	.0753
0.2	.0793	.0832	.0871	.0910	.0948	.0987	.1026	.1064	.1103	.1141
0.3	.1179	.1217	.1255	.1293	.1331	.1368	.1406	.1443	.1480	.1517
0.4	.1554	.1591	.1628	.1664	.1700	.1736	.1772	.1808	.1844	.1879
0.5	.1915	.1950	.1985	.2019	.2054	.2088	.2123	.2157	.2190	.2224
0.6	.2257	.2291	.2324	.2357	.2389	.2422	.2454	.2486	.2517	.2549
0.7	.2580	.2611	.2642	.2673	.2704	.2734	.2764	.2794	.2823	.2852
0.8	.2881	.2910	.2939	.2967	.2995	.3023	.3051	.3078	.3106	.3133
0.9	.3159	.3186	.3212	.3238	.3264	.3290	.3315	.3340	.3365	.3389
1.0	.3413	.3438	.3461	.3485	.3508	.3531	.3554	.3577	.3599	.3621
1.1	.3643	.3665	.3686	.3708	.3729	.3749	.3770	.3790	.3810	.3830
1.2	.3849	.3869	.3888	.3907	.3925	.3944	.3962	.3980	.3997	.4015
1.3	.4032	.4049	.4066	.4082	**.4099**	.4115	.4131	.4147	.4162	.4177
1.4	.4192	.4207	.4222	.4236	.4251	.4265	.4279	.4292	.4306	.4319
1.5	.4332	.4345	.4357	.4370	.4383	.4394	.4406	.4418	.4429	.4441
1.6	.4452	.4463	.4474	.4484	.4495	.4505	.4515	.4525	.4535	.4545
1.7	.4554	.4564.	4573	.4582	.4591	.4599	.4608	.4616	.4625	.4633
1.8	.4641	.4649	.4656	.4664	.4671	.4678	.4686	.4693	4699	.4706
1.9	.4713	.4719	.4726	.4732	.4738	.4744	.4750	.4756	.4761	.4767
2.0	.4772	.4778	.4783	.4788	.4793	.4798	.4803	.4808	.4812	.4817
2.1	.4821	.4826	.4830	.4834	.4838	.4842	.4846	.4850	.4854	.4857
2.2	.4861	.4864	.4868	.4871	.4875	.4878	.4881	.4884	.4887	.4890
2.3	.4893	.4896	.4898	.4901	.4904	.4906	.4909	.4911	.4913	.4916
2.4	.4918	.4920	.4922	.4925	.4927	.4929	.4931	.4932	.4934	.4936
2.5	.4938	.4940	.4941	.4943	.4945	.4946	.4948	.4949	.4951	.4952
2.6	.4953	.4955	.4956	.4957	.4959	.4960	.4961	.4962	.4963	.4964
2.7	.4965	.4966	.4967	.4968	.4969	.4970	.4971	.4972	.4973	.4974
2.8	.4974	.4975	.4976	.4977	.4977	.4978	.4979	4979	.4980	.4981
2.9	.4981	4982	4982	.4983	.4984	.4984	.4985	.4985	.4986	.4986
3.0	.4987	.4987	.4987	.4988	.4988	.4989	.4989	.4989	.4990	.4990

Figure 4.6.   Percent of Total Area under the Normal Curve

times they are not. We need to be able to identify distributions that are called *skewed*, or not normally distributed. (See Figure 2.4 in chapter 2.)

Just as a review, *normal distribution curves* have the following characteristics:

- They are unimodal—having one mode only.
- The maximum height is at the mean where the zero (0) or vertical axis touches the top of the curve.
- The mean, median, and mode are equal.
- They are symmetrical and bell-shaped. One half approximates the other half, a mirror image.
- There are one-half of the scores on one side and one-half on the opposite side of the mean.

- There are three standard deviations above and below the mean.
- They assume an infinite number of scores underneath the curve so the two tails at either end do not touch the abscissa.
- They can be either platykurtic (flat) or leptokurtic (peaked), as well as in between.

On the other hand, we could have *positively or negatively skewed distributions*. How do we know? If scores are clustered near the middle in a frequency distribution with a few scores at the high and low ends, then it is pretty much a normal distribution. If there are concentrations of scores on either the high or low ends, then the distribution is skewed. Here are the hints.

- Our frequency distributions will confirm this because they will have outliers in them.
- The mean, median, and mode will not be equal.
- The frequency polygon will extend outward either left of right. This extension is called a *tail.*

POSITIVELY SKEWED DISTRIBUTIONS

The *tail* of the curve tells you what kind of skew you have. If the tail is to the right, you have a *positively skewed curve.* With a positively skewed curve, the hump of the curve is toward the left. Remember when graphing frequency polygons, the left side of the horizontal axis begins with the lowest scores. Because the hump is in this vicinity, your distribution has many low scores. The few high scores, represented in the tail area, skew it. These "outlier" high scores pull the mean upward; the average is over-represented. The mean *shifts* toward the outlier. In a positively skewed distribution, the mode is at the peak of the distribution. The mean is off to the right and the median is in between.

An example of a positively skewed distribution would be scores on a very difficult test where only a few students did well. The few that did well would be the scores on the tail and those who did not do well would be the large hump. A science class exam might have this type of distribution. Sometimes, this type of curve exists when educators are selecting a few students for a special program such as a gifted program for budding writers. Those in the tail of the curve would qualify or be selected because the program targets outliers—students with an extremely high aptitude for writing.

NEGATIVELY SKEWED DISTRIBUTIONS

If the tail is to the left, you have a *negatively skewed curve*. With a negatively skewed curve, the hump or curve shows where most students' scores are falling. In this case they are at the higher end of the horizontal axis: the hump or curve is on the right side of the frequency polygon. The few low scores, represented in the tail area, skew it. These "outlier" low scores pull the mean downward; the average is under-represented. The mean *shifts* toward the outlier. In a negatively skewed distribution, the mode remains at the peak, the mean is off to the left and the median is in between.

An example of a negatively skewed distribution would be scores on an easy test where most did well. A driver's education exam should have a negatively skewed distribution. Most people pass it. This could also be the distribution of your school's reading scores where most should be proficient. Negatively skewed distributions may be used to identify those students who need remediation. You would be looking at those scores in the tail to identify students with high levels of need.

CHAPTER SUMMARY

Reporting only part of the story about your data set occurs when measures for variance are missing. You are looking at part of the information puzzle, but leaving off an important dimension. If decisions hinge on these descriptive statistics, then using both central tendency measures and measures of variation will be considered vital.

Chapter Five

Drawing a Sample to Represent the Whole Group

Time is at premium in the school setting. Although it probably was never conceived in this fashion, statistics is a tool for time management. It allows you to build an information base without spending many extra hours. Why is this so?

Statistics are based on samples. We have often heard the terms "random sample" or "scientific sample." Yet, few of us really know what this designation means or understand how valuable it is.

POPULATIONS AND SAMPLES

"Population" makes us think of people in our town, region, state, or country and their respective characteristics such as gender, age, marital status, ethnic membership, religion, and so forth. In statistics, the term *population* takes on a slightly different meaning.

The *population* in statistics includes all members of a defined group that we are studying or collecting information on. The operative descriptor is "all"—all students, all grade levels, all faculty members, all parents, or the entire community of households in whatever geographic circle we are focused on. This could be our school district, our city or town, our region, our state, or our nation. So the *population* in our statistical study is defined by the "who" (target group) and the "where" (the geographic boundary that this group exists in).

A *part* of the population is called a *sample*. Samples are studied to obtain valuable information about the larger group called the population. Once we define our population, we can take a sample of the population to conduct our statistics. A sample is a subset or subgroup of our population. It is a proportion of the population, a slice of it, a part of it, and all its characteristics. A sample is a scientifically drawn group that actually *possesses the same characteristics* as the population—if it is drawn randomly. This may be hard for you to believe, but it is true.

Randomly drawn samples must have two characteristics:

- Every person has an equal opportunity to be selected for the sample.
- Selection of one person is independent of the selection of another person.

We use samples all of the time to represent the whole. We take a sample of exotic food—maybe a bite or two—to see if it pleases our palette. We use a sample of new software that comes in the mail to see if it really works as well as the manufacturer purports it does. We take a sample of client references to see if the consultant is as good as the proposal suggests. We visit a sample of classrooms to determine if behavioral issues are increasing. We sample some of the households in our community to see what languages are spoken at home.

WHY SAMPLE?

Why not use the entire population to draw our conclusions? The short answer is it is a waste of time and money. For most purposes, we can obtain suitable accuracy—quickly and inexpensively—from a sample. Assessing all individuals may be impossible, impractical, expensive, or even inaccurate. It is usually not feasible to include an *entire* population in a study except if the number of those in our population is small and manageable. Furthermore, statistics make it unnecessary. A sign of ineptitude in data management is using an entire population when a sample will provide the same results. You save money, time, make fewer mistakes, and achieve the same end.

What is great about random samples is that you can generalize to the population that you are interested in. So if you sample 500 households in your community, you can generalize to the 50,000 households that live there. If you match some of the demographic characteristics of the 500 with the 50,000, you will see that they are surprisingly similar. Technically speaking, if you calculated a mean for these 500 randomly selected households and then draw another sample of 500 different households from the same population as the first, your means would be the same. This is the beauty of random samples. If drawn scientifically, they represent the entire population which you are interested in.

Many doubting Thomases will still be skeptical about whether a sample can truly represent the population. This is understandable. Yet, if properly conducted, sampling does work. Think about all of the polls done during political elections. They do not survey *all* of the nation's households. Instead, a random sample is drawn and surveyed. The results are pretty accurate. If you would like to get a feeling for the size of samples that represent entire populations, please refer to Krejcie and Morgan (1970). Table 5.1 suggests the great benefit that randomly selected samples afford educators. The larger the population size, the smaller the sample. However, for smaller samples, you must use almost the entire population. (Population size is noted by N and sample size by n.)

Table 5.1.   Random Sample Sizes (n)
Required for Population (N) Representation

Population Size (N)	Sample Size (n)
50	44
100	80
500	217
1,000	278
1,500	306
3,000	341
5,000	357
10,000	375
50,000	381
100,000	384

Samples must be drawn according to scientific principles and with precision and accuracy. There is always a price; to have a *truly representative* sample, you need to pay the piper. But the process is quite simple and methodological. If you follow the steps, you will find that the characteristics of your population are the same as those that your sample possesses. This is a good check on the validity of your sample. If the percentages on some of the demographics are known about your population, then the same demographics will appear in the sample. This is a good test and a very convincing piece of information for those skeptics.

As a note, statistics conducted on populations are called *parameters* and are designated with Greek letters. Statistics calculated on samples are called *statistics* and have Latin or Roman letters ascribed to them.

STEPS FOR DRAWING SIMPLE RANDOM SAMPLES

There is a method to the madness when sampling and you must abide by the rules in order for your sample to be representative of the population.

- *The first step in drawing a random sample is to identify all of the members in your population.* You must be able to list them in what is called a *sampling frame.* The frame should have the names without order to them and there should be no overlapping (no duplicates). Alphabetizing the list by surname is a way to insure a random order in the sampling frame. Your computer can sort alphabetically based on the last name, if surname is entered into a database as a separate field. One reason that you need to insure random order of names is that some lists cluster names by neighborhood location, housing type, income or some other grouping. This precludes their "equal chance" of being selected.

- *Second, you must give each name an identification number.* Start with "1" and continue.

- *Third, you must decide the size for your sample.* You can use the table, suggested in the Krejcie and Morgan (1970) article, or whatever you believe is right in order to believe in the results you obtain. As a rule of thumb, use as large a sample as possible. Whenever you are calculating means, percentages, or other statistics, the population is being estimated. Statistics calculated from large samples are more accurate than those from small samples. Large samples give the principle of randomness a chance to work.

- *Fourth, you need to get a* Table of Random Numbers. (Figure 5.1 displays a partial one). Many are located at the end of statistical or mathematical textbooks or online. The Table of Random Numbers contains numbers generated mechanically so that there is no discernable order of system to them. Each digit gets an equal representation. The Table of Random Numbers consist of rows and columns of numbers arranged at random so that they can be used as any point by reading in any direction left or right, up or down.

We are now ready to draw our random sample.

A SIMPLE EXAMPLE

Here is our sampling frame of 20 members of our population—let's say our fourth grade classroom. We want to draw a random sample of 5 students who will go on a special field trip with other fourth graders from other schools to meet a well-known children's author. We have listed all 20 students in our fourth grade class in alphabetical order and assigned an ID number to each from 1 through 20.

Sampling Frame
ID Name
1. Annie
2. Ellen
3. Emily
4. Estelle
5. James
6. Jessica
7. Joey
8. Juan
9. Julia
10. Katherine
11. Lia
12. Mary
13. Loren
14. Mande
15. McKenzie
16. Michelle
17. Miguel
18. Olivia
19. Raphael
20. Rebecca

We know that our largest ID number has two digits (20). So we are going to need a two-digit column in the Table of Random Numbers. We close our eyes and put our finger down any place in the Table of Random Numbers. This is our starting point. We have decided in advance whether we would use two digits going up, down, left, or right. So we begin.

In Figure 5.1, we have a sample from a Table of Random Numbers—just for the point of illustration. In boldface is our starting point of 37. We do not have an ID number that is 37 and so we proceed down: 37, 81, 89, and we come to 06.

ID Number #6 is the first ID number that is within our band of between 1 and 20. This is the first member of our random sample and it is *Jessica*. We continue 82, 56, 96, 66, 46 until we come up with the next ID—#13 *Loren*.

Our three last members of the sample are ID #8 (*Juan*), ID #5 (*James*), and ID #4 (*Estelle*). We have five randomly selected members: Jessica, Loren, Juan, James and Estelle.

53	74	23	99	67	61	32	28	69	84	94	62	67	86	24
63	38	06	86	54	99	00	65	26	94	02	82	90	23	07
35	30	58	21	46	06	72	17	10	94	25	21	31	75	96
63	43	36	82	69	65	51	18	**37**	88	61	38	44	12	45
98	25	37	55	26	01	91	82	81	46	74	71	12	94	97
02	63	21	17	69	71	50	80	89	56	38	15	70	11	48
64	55	22	21	82	48	22	28	**06**	00	61	54	13	43	91
85	07	26	13	89	01	10	07	82	**04**	59	63	69	36	03
58	54	16	24	15	51	54	44	82	00	62	61	65	04	69
34	85	27	84	87	61	48	64	56	26	90	18	48	13	26
03	92	18	27	46	57	99	16	96	56	30	33	72	85	22
62	95	30	27	59	37	75	41	66	48	86	97	80	61	45
08	45	93	15	22	60	21	75	46	91	98	77	27	85	42
07	08	55	18	40	45	44	75	**13**	90	24	94	96	61	02
01	85	89	95	66	51	10	19	34	88	15	84	97	19	75
72	84	71	14	35	19	11	58	49	26	50	11	17	17	76
88	78	28	16	84	13	52	53	94	53	75	45	69	30	96
45	17	75	65	57	28	40	19	72	12	25	12	74	75	67
96	76	28	12	54	22	01	11	94	25	71	96	16	16	88
43	31	67	72	30	24	02	94	**08**	63	38	32	36	66	02
50	44	66	44	21	66	06	58	**05**	62	68	15	54	35	02
22	66	22	15	86	26	63	75	41	99	58	42	36	72	24
96	24	40	14	51	23	22	30	88	57	95	67	47	29	83
31	73	91	61	19	60	20	72	93	48	98	57	07	23	69
78	60	73	99	84	43	89	94	36	45	56	69	47	07	41

Figure 5.1. Table of Random Numbers

THE OLD WAY WORKS, TOO

For such a small sampling frame, we could have done it the old way by drawing 5 names out of a hat that had all 20 names in it. You can draw a random sample that way instead of using the Table of Random Numbers. You simply put all names in a container and thoroughly mix them up. If you have 1,000 names in the bowl and want a sample of 100, draw the first name out. That is the first person in the sample. Mix up the names. (If you don't do this, then the name at the bottom will have less of a chance of being selected.) After mixing, draw the next name and continue until you get 100. This works the exact same way as using the Table of Random Numbers and is useful if your sample is small in size.

OTHER USEFUL SAMPLING STRATEGIES

Simple random sampling is the premier way to draw your sample. Other sampling strategies are very useful as well. Many books on sampling provide more in-depth information about the processes and the benefits. Here is a summary of a few procedures that educators can consider.

Systematic sampling is an often-used sampling strategy that's cost effective. Again, you must have a population sampling frame list that is in random order and non-overlapping. Determine both the size of the population and the size of the sample you want to work with. Then, divide the sample size (n) into the population (N) size to get your key number, symbolized as k.

- For example, if you had a population of 1,500 (N) and needed to have a sample of 306 (n), the key number (k) would be 5.
- Then, you would randomly pick any number between 1 and 5. Let's say you picked "4." That is your first ID number. Whoever is ID #4 is the first member of your sample from the list of 1,500.
- Then, systematically add 5 (your key number) to the first ID number of 4 and you get #9. ID #9 is the second member of your sample.
- The next ID number is ID #14, then ID #19, ID#24, ID#29 until you get your sample size up to the 306 you intended.

You might use systematic sampling to select a sample of households in your community for a community survey. The city hall might have the listing already available, in random order and with ID numbers in sequence. This saves you time and labor. If the city hall will give you a set of mailing labels, then it will be all the better.

Cluster sampling is exactly what its title implies. You randomly select clusters or groups in a population instead of individuals. This would work if a state wanted to sample all third graders on their writing skills. They would randomly select third grade classrooms from all third grade class-rooms in the state. Each of those classrooms selected would have 100% of the students in that classroom in the sample. The sampling unit or cluster is the third grade classroom not the individual student. Sometimes, this is a more practical effort than selecting individuals. Each member of the cluster has an equal chance of being selected. The random selection of the clusters provides estimates of the population. This is a good cost reduction technique.

Stratified sampling is used when the population is heterogeneous and it is important to represent the different strata or sub-populations. There is a proportional representation of strata in the sample—proportional to the popu-lation strata. We divide the entire population into strata (groups) to obtain groups of people that are more or less equal in some respect. Then, select a random sample from each stratum. This insures that no group is missed and improves the precision of our estimates. This might be used with dif-ferent racial/ethnic groups if we wanted to insure that our sample included a proportional representation of African Americans, Asians, and Latinos in addition to the Caucasians that pre-dominated our demographic pool in the school district.

Convenience samples, exactly what the name suggests, are oftentimes what we have to use because of reality. We cannot draw a sample, but we have a group that is accessible, is representative of our target popula-tion, and available to us. Instead of becoming purists and throwing out the chance for collecting data, use what you have with the honest acknowledge-ment that there are limitations. If you proceed to collect data with respect to some systematic, thoughtful process, it is better than throwing out the research altogether. For example, you may survey parents who attend the annual Parents' Open House at your middle school. Your school system cannot afford to conduct a mailed survey to all parent households in your system or draw a random sample of parent households. The open house provides an accessible and captive audience of parents from which you can extract some valuable information about perceptions, satisfaction levels, expectations and needs.

CHAPTER SUMMARY

Except when the population of interest is small, it is prudent to survey an entire population with the sampling procedures available. By using Simple Random, Systematic, Cluster, Stratified or even Convenience sampling procedures we can get a handle on what we need to know, and save time and limited fiscal/human resources. One of the most important uses of samples is that they afford us the opportunity to make inferences without spending a fortune in time and money to do so.

REFERENCE

Krejcie, R.V., & Morgan, D.W. (1970). Determining Sample Size for Research Activities. *Educational and Psychological Measurements*, *30*, 607–10.

Chapter Six

Putting Your Ideas and Assumptions to the Test

Descriptive statistics, which describe our data, are very useful to educators. Other statistics are also very useful, but take a little more expertise in implementation. They are called *inferential statistics*. This is because we can draw conclusions or inferences from them.

In the course of a work day, educators come up with guesses or hunches that they believe to be true about their students, parents, peers, and the community. In order to tell whether these hypotheses are true or false, they have to subject them to a test. They may draw a randomly selected sample from their population of interest, compute statistics on the sample, and test whether their hunch is true or false. The role of the sample, discussed in the previous chapter, is essential to the process and makes the task of inferring a possibility. The inferential statistics most commonly used to draw these conclusions include t-test, One-Way Analysis of Variance, chi-square analysis and correlational techniques among many others. These four will be discussed since they are considered to be user-friendly, pragmatic and applicable in educational settings. As a result, these are the most commonly used.

HYPOTHESIS TESTING

Hypotheses are suppositions presumed to be true. Investigations by educators that test well-conceived hypotheses can yield evidence of considerable importance. They can tell us whether we should switch from one instructional method to another. They can tell us the degree to which having breakfast impacts learning for elementary school students. They can document the value of getting more males to participate in extracurricular activities. They can tell us whether Smarter Balanced test scores are improving, declining or staying the same from year to year. They can answer many of our critical questions and turn hunches into strategic information upon which data based decisions can be made.

Because of the importance of posing these hypotheses, it is crucial to accept those that are true and reject those that are false. But how do we do this?

Central to the discussion of inferential statistics is the concept of probability. When your statistical analysis reveals that the probability is rare that the statistical result is due to chance, we call this a "statistically significant" result. It means that our observed outcome is so unique that it could not have occurred by chance alone.

NON-DIRECTIONAL AND DIRECTIONAL NULL HYPOTHESES

All research, whether it is in the classroom or in the laboratory, begins with the research question or hypothesis. It is always stated in the null (negative) and is called the *null hypothesis*. This is because you have to be able to prove something is indeed true. It is similar to the philosophy in the courtroom of proving someone guilty—innocent until proven guilty. The onus of proof is on the educator to prove that the null is true. Technically speaking, the word "hypothesis" is a Greek word that means "an assumption subject to verification."

Basically, there are two types of null hypotheses. The first type tests for *differences*. Two null hypotheses that test for differences are presented below as an illustration of how to state them correctly. Corresponding examples follow each. The second type of null hypothesis tests for *relationships* between two variables. One is presented as a way to state it correctly and there is a corresponding example.

NULL HYPOTHESES THAT TEST FOR DIFFERENCES

- There is *no difference* between two groups on variable X (as represented by their mean scores). Example: there is no difference between newly hired and tenured teachers on their teaching competence with respect to the Common Core State Standards.

- There is *no difference* among three or more groups on variable X (as represented by their mean scores). Example: there is no difference among Asian, African American, Hispanic, and Caucasian students with respect to performance on Smarter Balanced tests.

Sometimes a null hypothesis for differences takes a courageous step and predicts the direction of the difference. This is called a *directional null hypothesis*. Instead of stating a nondirectional null like this, "With respect to the Common Core State Standards, there is no difference in teaching competence between newly hired and tenured teachers," you would state a directional null like this, "With respect to the Common Core State Standards, teaching competence is greater for tenured than for newly hired teachers." The basis for this *directional* guess should be your knowledge base, evidence in the professional literature, or your own experience, and not a superficial guess. You are actually stating which mean score will be greater when you calculate your statistics.

In this case, you really believe that newly hired teachers have more competence than tenured teachers do with respect to the Common Core State Standards. Remember that the hypothesis must still be stated in the *opposite* of what you think is true. It has to be stated in the null—which you really think is false. Then you have to prove it to be false. When we accept the null (or fail to reject the null), we are saying that our results are not statistically significant and are due to chance. When we reject the null (or the null is false) we are saying that our results are statistically significant and due to factors or conditions other than chance.

NULL HYPOTHESES THAT TEST FOR *RELATIONSHIPS*

There is *no relationship* between variable X and variable Y.

Example: There is no relationship between school attendance and academic performance.

For practical utility, this book will focus on these two types of null hypotheses—those that test for differences and those that test for relationships. The discussion is going to be kept simple yet practical so that you can use this information in your school system.

PROBABILITY LEVELS

Many events in life are inherently uncertain. Any event may or may not occur. Probability applies exclusively to the likely occurrence of a future event. In statistics, probability provides a quantitative measurement of the likelihood that an event will occur. In other words, probability is used to measure the certainty or uncertainty of the outcome of an event. If it is sure to occur, the probability is 1.00 or 100%. If it will never occur, the probability is 0.

A probability of .50 means the event should occur once in every two attempts or 50% of the time. So any event that may or may not occur has a probability of between 0 and 1.00.

Educational journals often state that the results are "statistically significant" or "the probability level is less than .05." This means that observed difference is likely to be real rather than by chance. Although somewhat arbitrary, the significance level (alpha) is the magnitude of error that one is willing to take in making the decision to reject the null hypothesis.

The conventional levels for rejecting the null hypothesis are either .05 or .01. One (.01) is more conservative than the other (.05) because with .01 you are less willing to have your results due to chance alone; you will accept only 1 time in 100 that your results were due to chance. A .05 level of statistical significance is more generous in accepting a statement as true. With this probability level you will accept 5 times in 100 that your results were due to chance. A very conservative probability level is .001. This may be used in scientific studies such as pharmaceutical efficacy. In education, the commonly accepted probability levels are .05 and .01.

As a note, you need to choose the probability level a priori. This is a Latin term meaning "in advance." You have to decide early on—before you collect your data—and accept it when your statistical testing is completed. It is unethical for us to choose the conservative .01 level and then find out that we would have had statistical significance if we were more liberal with a choice of .05.

TYPE I AND TYPE II ERRORS

The selection of probability levels comes with the chance of making errors. These are called Type I and Type II errors.

Type I

A Type I error is when you reject the null when it was actually true. We conclude falsely that there were differences when there was none. This can be problematic when someone else replicates our study and our results do not hold up!

Making a Type I error is based on the level of statistical significance. If you selected .05, then 5 times out of 100 your results will be due to chance. Unfortunately, you got one of the five times. A more conservative level is .01 where only one time out of 100 your results will be due to chance alone. A liberal level is .10 where you feel that 10 times out of 100 chance results are OK with you. This level is not often selected in educational settings and can largely contribute to Type I errors.

Type I errors may be costly to your school. If you are thinking about switching to a new instructional curriculum with requisite text purchases and teacher training, your decision can be very expensive in tax dollars. Besides impairing your image, the new investment was really ineffective. Your decision to change from the status quo was wrong. This may be avoided by using a more conservative level of statistical significance. This is advised if the decision has great implications for your school district.

Type II

A Type II error occurs when you accept the null when it was in fact false. We conclude that there are no differences when in fact there were! This is less costly in educational settings because you are maintaining the status quo. If you should have rejected the null but did not, the maintenance of the status quo may be a mistake. If you maintain the status quo, but have a new idea that really makes a difference, children can suffer. If you used a conservative probability level to determine if school breakfast had an effect on academic performance for your kindergarten class, you may be keeping kids hungry and having them learn less because of your error in design. Figure 6.1 summarizes what happens.

	ACCEPT the NULL↓	REJECT the NULL↓
The hypothesis is true.→	You are right!	You committed a Type I error. Probability level is more liberal (.05).
The hypothesis is false. →	You committed a Type II error. Probability level is more conservative (.01).	You are right!

Figure 6.1.

As a note, the only way to know that you have a Type I or Type II error in your findings is through replication. All good studies are repeated in order to corroborate findings. This may not be feasible in educational settings, but trying to insure good research practices "by the book" is always the goal and in everyone's best interest.

ONE-TAILED AND TWO-TAILED TESTS
OF STATISTICAL SIGNIFICANCE

With nondirectional null hypotheses, educators are only suggesting that there will be a difference in mean score results. Which of the scores will be higher is not speculated upon. In the case of a nondirectional null hypothesis, a two-tailed test of significance is used.

If there is a prediction of which mean will be higher and which will be lower, then a one-tailed test of significance is used. When you state a directional hypothesis, a one-tailed test of significance is used (Figure 6.2).

Non-directional null hypothesis ⟶ *Two-tailed test of significance*

Directional null hypothesis ⟶ *One-tailed test of significance*

Figure 6.2.

This may seem like a lot of mumbo jumbo, but all it means is simply this. A directional hypothesis is a serious commitment for someone to make; they are predicting which mean score of the groups they are comparing is higher or lower. (The mean score of newly hired teachers will be higher than the mean score of tenured teachers.) When you choose this, you are rewarded with a one-tailed test of statistical significance. What this means is that your ability to reject the null is boosted or heightened. The ability to reject the null is called *power*—power to reject the null.

FACTORS CONTRIBUTING TO "POWER"

There are certain conditions where it is easier to reject the null hypothesis.

1. *If you use parametric statistics.* Parametric statistics are the elite statistics. They are more powerful than non-parametric statistics in rejecting the null. But they depend on meeting a few assumptions before you use them. They work best if your distribution is not skewed but rather a normal, bell shaped, and symmetrical distribution. The groups that you are comparing should have equal variances or spread. This is called *homogeneity of variance*.

Parametric statistics that will be discussed in this primer are t-tests, One Way Analysis of Variance, and Pearson Product Moment correlation techniques.

These are more powerful tests to reject the null hypothesis. Also, they are described as *robust*, a statistical term which means that they can hold up even when the assumptions stated above are violated. Parametric statistics rely on the computation of means and standard deviations, which use interval and ratio scaling.

Non-parametric statistics require that you meet very few assumptions. They do not require normal distributions or equal variances. They are oftentimes based on ordinal or nominal measurement and are easier to compute. They use frequency counts instead of complicated calculations. Because non-parametric statistics do not always rely on means and standard deviations, they lack the precision that parametric statistics possess. Generally speaking, if you know that the data come from a population that is normally distributed you should use the parametric test. If not, use the non-parametric test. In chapter 9, we will discuss chi-square analysis as an essential non-parametric statistic for use in educational settings.

2. *If you use a directional hypothesis.* One-tailed tests (used with directional null hypotheses) are more powerful than two-tailed tests (used with non-directional hypotheses).

3. *If you use large sample sizes.* These are more powerful than small sample sizes.

4. *If you use a more liberal probability level.* If you choose .05 instead of .01, your chances to reject the null are greater.

5. *If you use superior measurement tools* that are documented to have high reliability and validity, attributes of good instruments.

STEPS—HYPOTHESIS TESTING OR IMPLEMENTING THE SCIENTIFIC PROCESS

The following four steps constitute the basis for scientific inquiry, hypothesis testing. This framework may be more conceptual than practiced since computer programs have taken some of the work out of the steps. Yet it is a risky but common practice for some schools to use high-powered statistical packages with very little understanding of the processes involved. Familiarity and awareness are essential for conducting any inferential statistical procedure. This book is based on that premise and will present the inferential statistics in that spirit in the next four chapters.

1. *State the hypothesis in the null form.* The null can be stated for either differences or relationships. If for differences, the null is either non-directional or directional, but you must be aware of which type you are using.

2. *Select your level of significance* or level of probability, either .05 or .01. *.05* establishes a 95% confidence level and is more liberal. *.01* establishes a 99% confidence level and is more conservative.

3. *Compute your statistical analysis.* Determine whether you have a statistically significant result. (How this is done will be discussed in detail in the next few chapters.)

No statistically significant result: accept your null as true.

Yes, a statistically significant result: reject your null as false.

4. *Determine the educational significance of your results.* Is the statistical difference meaningful? Or is this a "so what?" finding. Concerning the last step, don't let your ego overtake common sense.

Wise educators must look beyond statistical significance when making data driven decisions and ask themselves, "Is this educationally significant?" Is the difference between the two or more mean scores large enough to be worth the cost of changing curriculum, eliminating a course or adding a new textbook? How important is the difference? How much better can this finding make our school or school district? Is the change worth it? What is the cost effectiveness? Are the gains in student scores large enough to invest in to obtain this difference? This is the last step in hypothesis testing and one that we have to put our egos aside to answer for the good of our schools.

A final thought is in order regarding statistical significance. Everyone seems to think that getting a statistically significant result is the "golden ring." This is not always the case. It depends on what you are asking in your evaluation or research study. For example, if you want to know if males and females have different attitudes toward mathematics, you would like to think there was no significant difference. If you were asking whether there were differences in teaching expertise between newly hired and tenured teachers, you would like to think there was none.

CHAPTER SUMMARY

The use of inferential statistics in educational settings allows us to make strategic decisions based on data. We avoid guessing, speculating, and listening to the squeaky wheels about what is effective, what is not, what should stay in the budget, what should be eliminated, what should be added or expanded, what should be changed or modified. Inferential statistics go a long way toward supplying the foundation for smart decisions. There is a price. A method to the madness must be observed. There is a scientific nature to hypothesis testing and principles that must be respected. But it is a small price to pay for what schools get in exchange.

Chapter Seven

t-Tests: Examining Differences between Two Groups

For educators, many decisions are focused on comparisons.

To determine which method of instruction has a greater impact on student
performance.
To compare professional development modules to see which ones teachers
value more.
To assess Smarter Balanced performance in two seventh grades in your district.

When two groups are compared, the statistic that is most useful is very often
the t-test. It is both an inferential and a parametric statistic.

The purpose of a t-test is to determine if there is a statistically significant
difference between the *mean* scores of two groups. This is where the mean,
the queen of central tendency, is vital. The mean scores of two groups are
compared via the formula for a t-test. Because the t-test is a parametric statistic, it is powerful. If there are differences, even slight ones, the t-test will
uncover them.

There are a few basic facts about t-tests:

1. A t-test is used if there are only *two* groups to compare.

2. This statistical technique answers the null hypothesis: there *is no difference* between two groups on their respective mean scores.

3. There is one Independent variable with two (2) categories and there is one
Dependent variable.

INDEPENDENT AND DEPENDENT VARIABLES

There is much confusion about what constitutes independent and dependent variables. To understand the difference is fundamental to executing statistics properly. This is where the use of a statistical software package can be dangerous if you are not aware of even the basic content presented in this primer. The simplicity of "click, click" superficially erases the need to know. But understanding which one is the dependent and which one is the independent variable is vital to producing correct statistical analysis.

The *Independent variable*—input, manipulated, treatment variable—is independent of the outcome but presumed to cause, effect, or influence the outcome. The D*ependent variable*—outcome, response variable—is dependent on the Independent variable; the outcome depends on how the independent variables are manipulated or managed. So an Independent variable might be gender and the Dependent variable might be attitudes toward science, technology, engineering, and math (STEM) careers. You might administer a survey to determine whether there are different attitudes toward STEM careers for eighth graders. You have classified students by gender—manipulated the variable instead of using boys and girls combined—to see its impact on STEM attitudes.

Basically, the independent variable for a t-test is nominally scaled. There are two discrete categories with one variable. It is that simple. Many educators think that because there are two categories, there are two independent variables. There is only one independent variable with a t-test and it has two categories. Table 7.1 presents a few examples.

Table 7.1.

Independent Variable	Group 1 Category	Group 2 Category
Senior college placement	Private colleges	Public colleges
Third graders	Readers	Non-readers
Seventh graders	Band member	Choral member
Gender	Male	Female
Parents/Guardians	GED/Diploma	No GED/Diploma
Faculty	Chemistry	Biology
Preschoolers	Hispanic	Non-Hispanic
School Staff	Paraprofessionals	Teachers
Community	Year-round residents	Summer home residents

To nominally scale these independent variables for statistical analysis in a t-test, you can assign a "1" to one group and a "2" to the other. Remember, with nominal variables the numbers are only labels. They mean nothing in terms of measurement but everything in differentiating the categories of your independent variable.

With a t-test there is also only one dependent variable. It is continuous in its numeric range and uses either interval or ratio measurement scales. Sometimes, educators will use ordinal scales; it is not the perfect scenario given the parametric nature of the t-test, but the practice is common and acceptable. (See chapter 1 for a refresher on the different measurement scales.)

Common examples of dependent variables in educational settings are test scores, discipline offenses, attendance, dropout rates, parent satisfaction levels, organizational climate, student attitudes and teacher retention.

PRELIMINARY ASSUMPTIONS

In the last chapter, parametric statistics were described. This group of statistics is more powerful than non-parametric statistics in rejecting the null. But they depend on your meeting a few assumptions before you use them. Since the t-test is a parametric statistic, there are a few preliminary steps that you must abide by before you implement this statistical procedure.

- *The two groups should have equal variances on the dependent variable.* The variability (discussed in chapter 4) of the individual groups' mean scores must be equivalent. They must have the same degree of variability. This is called *a test of homogeneity of variance* and should be done as a preliminary step, a kind of insurance program for your data. This is particularly true when your groups are of different sizes (*n*)— common in educational settings (versus laboratory settings where things are "perfect").

- *The two groups should have an equal number of subjects.* If the two groups are unequal—like 20% more scores in one group than in the other, look at the standard deviation. If they are similar, go ahead and use the t-test. If it is not, use the Mann-Whitney U test, a non-parametric counterpart, discussed at the end of this chapter.

- *Groups should be equivalent on all other variables except the dependent variables.* For example, if you are examining instructional approaches in two elementary schools by comparing their performance test scores, make sure that the two elementary schools are similar on other characteristics. These might include income of the households that compose the feeder neighborhoods, percentages of students in special education, and other factors that may account for differences in test scores between the two schools instead of your focus—instructional approach.

In your effort to meet the assumptions of the t-test, keep in mind that t-tests are "robust." They can hold up even when the assumptions, stated above, are violated. Although this "robustness" lets us off the hook to some extent, it is a good idea to approximate to the greatest extent possible the rules of the game—the assumptions. This will insure excellent data management, avoid errors, and ultimately produce sound data.

STEPS FOR CONDUCTING A t-TEST

This example will help to explain the basic purpose of the t-test. (Even though there are software programs to click on for a t-test, you should be aware of the process so that you can ensure quality control over the results.)

You are the head of a large school district with 30 math teachers. Your K–8 teachers and those 9–12 were compared on the Learning Mathematics for Teaching (LMT), an instrument used to assess teachers' content knowledge as it related to the Common Core State Standards. You wondered if there was a difference between the two groups. This would have important implications for professional development, if found to be true. So you decide to compare the scores between the two groups of teachers.

Step One: You state your null hypothesis. It is non-directional.

There is no difference in mathematics knowledge between K–8 and 9–12 teachers.

Step Two: You identify your independent variable and your dependent variable.

"Teachers" was your independent variable with two categories—K–8 and 9–12 teachers. You took the listing of all of your teachers and separated them into the two groups. Group 1 was the K–8 group and Group 2 was the 9–12 group. Using nominal scaling, you assign each group a numeric label so that your t-test could be calculated. You used "1" and "2" as your numeric values, which represented the two categories of teachers.

Your Dependent variable was mathematics knowledge base, as measured by the LMT. You listed the score for each teacher on the mathematics test. You also calculated the mean scores for each of the two groups. The mean scores *appeared* different, but you could not really tell just from "eyeballing the data." A t-test formula had to be applied to the data to determine whether there is a statistically significant difference.

Step Three: You set up your data for data entry into a database.

The data for your t-test was recorded in a database such as that in Figure 7.1. As a note, you will be using *only the numeric values* in your database—that is the teachers' ID numbers, the Group codes, and the Mathematics scores for each of the teachers. This way, the name of the teacher is preserved for confidentiality. You have data on fifteen K–8 and fifteen 9–12 teachers.

ID	9-12 Teachers	Category N=30	Group code	LMT Score
1	Ms. Ramirez	9-12	1	88
2	Ms. Olsen	9-12	1	89
3	Ms. Sullivan	9-12	1	88
4	Ms. Considine	9-12	1	89
5	Ms. Dressel	9-12	1	76
6	Ms. Marchand	9-12	1	89
7	Mr. Ross	9-12	1	88
8	Ms. Beyer	9-12	1	89
9	Ms. Gallagher	9-12	1	88
10	Ms. Magistrali	9-12	1	89
11	Ms. Strand	9-12	1	89
12	Mr. Fischer	9-12	1	88
13	Ms. Bowen	9-12	1	89
14	Ms. Peak	9-12	1	88
15	Mrs. Pacheco	9-12	1	89
	Mean for Group 1	**15=n**		**87.73**

ID	K-8 Teachers	Category N=30	Group code	LMT Score
1	Ms. French	K-8	2	89
2	Mr. Dickinson	K-8	2	78
3	Ms. Addazio	K-8	2	75
4	Ms. Saidel	K-8	2	78
5	Mr. Dwyer	K-8	2	79
6	Ms. Zecca	K-8	2	89
7	Ms. Matarese	K-8	2	78
8	Ms. Kozlak	K-8	2	75
9	Mr. Fitz	K-8	2	78
10	Ms. Hernandez	K-8	2	79
11	Ms. Guzman	K-8	2	78
12	Ms. Santo	K-8	2	75
13	Ms. Strawson	K-8	2	78
14	Ms. Vega- Perez	K-8	2	79
15	Ms. Hebert	K-8	2	70
	Mean for Group 2	**15=n**		**78.53**

Figure 7.1. Two Groups of Teachers and their Mathematics Data for the LMT

Step Four: You execute the t-test statistical procedure to obtain a *calculated t-value.*

After you have entered your data from your database into the computer software program of your choice, you can execute the t-test procedure. You can also hand calculate the t-test by using a formula found in any statistics or mathematics textbook. Either way, the outcome is a t-value. It is called your *calculated t-value.*

For the sample data, your calculated t-value actually is –4.97. This calculated t-value is theoretically the calculated difference in your two mean scores in mathematics for the two groups of teachers. It is critical to your decision whether to reject or accept the null hypothesis. The t-value is a continuous number usually with two decimal places. The plus or minus sign in front of the t-value does not matter; ignore it.

Step Five: You compare your *calculated t-value* to the *critical t-value* in the t Distribution Table.

You have to compare your calculated t-value to what is called the critical t-value reported in the t Distribution Table usually found at the end of any research or statistics book, or on-line. A portion of this table is displayed in Figure 7.2. To use this table correctly you have to know three pieces of information.

- Was your null hypothesis a non-directional (two-tailed test) or a directional (one-tailed test) one?
- What was the level of probability that you selected? .05? .01?
- Did you use an Independent or Correlated t-test, which relates to the degrees of freedom (df)? (To be discussed in more detail, shortly.)

If the calculated t-value exceeds (is higher than) the critical t-value in the t Distribution Table, you reject the null. You have a statistically significant difference. If not, you accept the null as true. For your data set, the calculated t-value was 4.97. Since you had a non-directional hypothesis, a probability level of .05, and an Independent t-test ($df = 28$), the critical value in the t Distribution Table was 2.048. (It is highlighted in Figure 7.2 so that you can see how it was located.) Your calculated value of 4.97 exceeded the table value.

Step Six: Accept or reject the null hypothesis.

Your calculated value exceeded the t Distribution Table value. You reject the null hypothesis.

There is a difference in mathematics knowledge between K–8 and 9–12 teachers.

You found that your 9–12 teachers had statistically higher mathematics scores. When you have a statistically significant finding, you report it with

df	Two tailed test at p< .05	Two tailed test at p< .01	One tailed test at P< .05	One tailed test at p< .01
1	12.706	63.657	6.314	31.821
2	4.303	9.925	2.920	6.965
3	3.182	5.841	2.353	4.541
4	2.776	4.604	2.132	3.747
5	2.571	4.032	2.015	3.365
6	2.447	3.707	1.943	3.134
7	2.365	3.499	1.895	2.998
8	2.306	3.355	1.860	2.896
9	2.262	3.250	1.833	2.831
10	2.228	3.169	1.812	2.764
11	2.201	3.106	1.796	2.718
12	2.179	3.055	1.782	2.681
13	2.160	3.012	1.771	2.650
14	**2.145**	2.977	1.761	2.624
15	2.131	2.947	1.753	2.602
16	2.120	2.921	1.746	2.583
17	2.110	2.898	1.740	2.567
18	2.101	2.878	1.734	2.552
19	2.093	2.861	1.729	2.539
20	2.086	2.845	1.725	2.528
21	2.080	2.831	1.721	2.518
22	2.074	2.819	1.717	2.508
23	2.069	2.807	1.714	2.500
24	2.064	2.797	1.711	2.492
25	2.060	2.787	1.708	2.485
26	2.056	2.779	1.706	2.479
27	2.052	2.771	1.703	2.473
28	**2.048**	2.763	1.701	2.467
29	2.045	2.756	1.699	2.462
30	2.042	2.750	1.697	2.457

2.048= Table value for **Independent** Samples t-test

2.145= Table value for **Correlated** Samples t-test

Figure 7.2.   Distribution Table for t-Values

an asterisk. One asterisk (*) indicates that the probability level was .05, two asterisks (**) signify a probability level of .01, and the notation of NS usually stands for not statistically significant.

This t-test finding motivated you, as the educational leader of your school district, to implement professional development in areas where K–8 teachers needed skills. You addressed this by designing seminars to be taken during the next school year. That is the practical action step that resulted from your t-test. A t-test was how you arrived at this data driven decision.

INDEPENDENT AND CORRELATED t-TESTS

Although this primer is intended to keep things as simple as possible, there is a critical addendum to the t-test discussion. There are two forms of the t-test. One is called the *Independent Samples* t-test and the other is called the *Correlated Samples* t-test, also referred to as a *Paired, Matched or Dependent Samples* t-test. In order to use the t Distribution Table correctly, you need to know whether you conducted an Independent or Correlated Samples t-test.

The Independent Samples t-test is quite simple to understand and identify. The two groups, such as the K–8 and 9–12 teachers, have *no relationship* to each other. They are independent of one another, hence the name Independent Samples t-test.

Conversely, Correlated Samples t-tests use two groups that have a connection or relationship to each other. With this built-in relationship, it is more likely that the mean scores of the two groups have a relationship, too. So, the Correlated Samples formula takes the inherent relationship into account, and helps to find a statistical significance—if there is one there. Here are the occasions when you are using *Correlated* t-tests:

1. *When you have two sets of scores on the same individuals*—in other words when the individuals are tested twice. Two groups of data are really the same individual with two scores on each person. Table 7.2 displays an example where the students are measured twice. For each student, the pair or dual scores compose the two groups of data needed for a t-test.

Correlated t-tests are used most often in educational settings for this purpose. It is of great benefit to educators who want to determine impact, efficacy and persistence over time. Some examples of when a correlated t-test might be used include the following:

Table 7.2.

	Pre-test	Post-test
Olivia	120	140
Joey	120	120
Luke	130	160
Mia	150	160

- When assessing the ability of a new instructional method to raise test scores.
- When measuring the impact of an innovative program on students' attitudes.
- When weighing the cost benefit of a novel approach on remediation.
- When tracking parental involvement from last year to this year.
- When monitoring the effect of professional development training on knowledge acquisition.

2. If you have *matched* your sample on some other variable so that the two groups are alike.

One of the primary tenets of the t-test is that the two groups you are studying are alike *except* for your dependent variable. You want to insure that something else (called extraneous variance or error) does not account for differences between the two groups instead of your dependent variable.

For example, look at the data set of teachers discussed previously. What might account for the difference in mathematics knowledge besides whether a teacher is K–8 or 9–12? The answers might be the years in teaching, the grade level, the amount of professional development, confidence with the subject area, attitude toward the profession, or other factors. If there were one particular factor that you felt might compromise your data, you might try to match the groups on that variable, so that they are equivalent except for the dependent variable you were exploring.

3. *When you have sets of twins that compose the two groups.*

More often in laboratory settings, but sometimes in educational settings, sets of twins are used to compose the two groups. This is because they are genetically similar. Then, data are collected on each twin, and the t-test is conducted between the data for Twin Group A and Twin Group B to see if statistical differences exist. Because the two groups of twins are obviously related, the Correlated t-test is used. Table 7.3 shows how twins would be split into the two groups for data analysis on IQ scores.

Table 7.3

Group A		IQ Score	Group B	IQ Score
Gupta	Twin A	100	Twin B	102
Tran	Twin A	101	Twin B	104
Perez	Twin A	111	Twin B	112
Murphy	Twin A	144	Twin B	144

MATCHED SAMPLES

Here is an example of a matched sample. Using the same set of data that we used in the t-test, the two teacher groups were matched on the number of professional development courses they had taken. As you can see in Figure 7.3, each teacher in Group 1 is matched with another teacher in Group 2 on the number of professional development courses that they took. For each ID number in Group 1 there is a member of Group 2 that has the exact same number of professional development courses. Ramirez with French, Olsen with Dickinson and all the way through, there were pairs of teachers with the same number of professional development courses in each of the two groups.

The number of professional development courses would not be entered into the t-test that you were calculating. It would insure that your groups of teachers were equivalent on this important variable (number of professional development courses) before you began to compare mathematics knowledge. Your null hypothesis is still focused on mathematics knowledge—not the number of professional development courses.

USING THE t DISTRIBUTION TABLE CORRECTLY: DEGREES OF FREEDOM

The t Distribution Table is the reason that you must know whether you used an Independent Samples or Correlated Samples t-test. To use the t Distribution Table correctly, you must know what your degrees of freedom (df) are. This is a prerequisite for using most statistical tables. There is a column where "df" is noted so that you can find the critical value. In this case of the t-test, it is the critical *t-value*.

Independent Sample and Correlated Sample have different "degree of freedom" associated with each t-test form.

ID	Teachers	Number of Professional Dev. courses	Group 1	Group code	Mathematics Score
1.	Mr. Ramirez	1	9-12	1	88
2.	Ms. Olsen	1	9-12	1	89
3.	Ms. Sullivan	2	9-12	1	88
4.	Ms. Considine	3	9-12	1	89
5.	Mr. Dressel	4	9-12	1	70
6.	Ms. Marchand	1	9-12	1	89
7.	Mr. Ross	4	9-12	1	88
8.	Ms. Beyer	5	9-12	1	89
9.	Ms. Gallagher	3	9-12	1	88
10.	Ms. Magistrali	4	9-12	1	89
11.	Ms. Strand	5	9-12	1	89
12.	Mr. Fischer	1	9-12	1	88
13.	Ms. Bowen	2	9-12	1	89
14.	Ms. Peak	2	9-12	1	88
15.	Ms. Pacheco	3	9-12	1	89

ID	Teachers	Number of Professional Dev. courses	Group 2	Group code	Mathematics Score
1.	Ms. French	1	K-8	2	89
2.	Mr. Dickinson	1	K-8	2	78
3.	Ms. Addazio	2	K-8	2	75
4.	Ms. Saidel	3	K-8	2	78
5.	Mr. Dwyer	4	K-8	2	79
6.	Ms. Zecca	1	K-8	2	89
7.	Ms. Matarese	4	K-8	2	78
8.	Ms. Kozlak	5	K-8	2	75
9.	Mr. Fitz	3	K-8	2	78
10.	Ms. Hernandez	4	K-8	2	79
11.	Ms. Guzman	5	K-8	2	78
12.	Ms. Santo	1	K-8	2	75
13.	Ms. Strawson	2	K-8	2	78
14.	Ms. Vega- Perez	2	K-8	2	79
15.	Ms. Hebert	3	K-8	2	70

Figure 7.3. Matched Groups of Teachers and Their Mathematics Data for the T-test

- If you use an Independent Samples t-test, the degrees of freedom are equal to the number in your total sample minus 2 or $(N - 2)$. So in the first example of K–8 and 9–12 teachers, the degrees of freedom would be 28 (or 30 teachers minus 2 = 28). For a non-directional hypothesis (two-tailed test) at the .05 level with 28 degrees of freedom, your calculated t-value had to exceed 2.048, the actual critical value in the t Distribution Table. It did with a t-value of 4.97.

- If you are using a Correlated Samples t-test, the degrees of freedom are equal to the number of pairs minus 1 (N of pairs – 1). In the second example of teachers, you used matched pairs on professional development courses; the degrees of freedom would be 14 (or 15 pairs – 1). For a two-tailed test at the .05 level with 14 degrees of freedom, the critical value your calculated value must exceed is actually 2.145. Please refer to highlighted number in Figure 7.2.

As you can see the critical value for the Correlated Samples t is larger than that for the Independent Samples t. This makes it more difficult to reject the null. Since the data for the groups are related, you have to insure that the difference you find is real, and not due to the relationship between the sets of data. So the bar is raised with Correlated t-tests; the critical value in the t Distribution Table is greater for this form of the t-test.

REPORTING t-TEST RESULTS IN A TABLE FORMAT

Figure 7.4 illustrates how you might report your t-test findings in a table format both in your report and in professional journals.

Independent Samples t-test

TEACHERS GROUPS	MEAN	(SD)	t value	df	p
9-12	87.33	(4.9)	4.97	28	.05*
K-8	78.53	(4.9)			

*p<.05

Correlated Samples t-test

TEACHERS GROUPS	MEAN	(SD)	t value	df	p
9-12	87.33	(4.9)	4.97	14	.05*
K-8	78.53	(4.9)			

*p<.05

Figure 7.4.   t-test Tables

NON-PARAMETRIC COUNTERPARTS

There are two non-parametric statistical procedures that answer the same question that the t-test does. If the assumptions mentioned in the beginning of this chapter couldn't be met, then you may want to consider using a non-parametric alternative. The Mann-Whitney U-test and the Wilcoxon Matched Pairs Signed Ranks test are the counterparts to the Independent and Correlated t-test, respectively. They are not bound by normal distributions or equal variances. They can be used with ordinal data or ranked data instead of interval/ratio scaling for the dependent measure. The down side is that they are not as powerful as the parametric t-tests in rejecting the null hypothesis.

CHAPTER SUMMARY

The t-test is very useful tools in educational settings. Many times we are comparing two groups of students, instructional methods, reading programs, teaching strategies, or staff in order to make a decision. The t-test is a simple and straightforward statistic that allows us to get beyond a frequency count. A group's mean score may look different from another mean score; or it may look the same. The litmus test for *statistically significant* two group comparisons is called the t-test. It is a tool that educators can use to make decisions confidently, and then take the appropriate action steps based on the results.

Chapter Eight

ANOVA: What if There Are More Than Two Groups?

The t-test is very handy when educators have two groups or testing times (pre/post) to compare. But what happens if you have more than two groups? The statistical technique that is analogous to the t-test is called Analysis of Variance, or ANOVA. The purpose of the ANOVA is understood quickly if it is thought of as an extension of the t-test.

The ANOVA is an inferential statistic. It is also a parametric statistic and as such, it is very powerful. It can reject the null or find differences among groups—if they exist. The assumptions of homogeneity of variance, equal group sizes, and normal distribution of scores should be adhered to—just as the t-test should meet these assumptions. Yet, as a robust statistic, ANOVA can sustain having the assumptions violated and still perform its function. There is a non-parametric version of the ANOVA called the Krusal-Wallis H test. If you have serious violations of the assumptions, use it.

Frankly, ANOVA is a little more complicated than a t-test and may require some outside expertise to execute and to interpret it (even with a statistical package). For the purpose of discussion, the main point is that you use ANOVA as you do a t-test—but *when there are more than two groups*. There is one Dependent and one Independent variable (but with more than two levels or categories). Although there are many versions of the ANOVA, this primer will focus on a simple version—the One-Way ANOVA.

Here are some facts about One-Way ANOVAs:

- This statistical technique answers the null hypothesis: there is *no difference* among three or more (3+) groups on their respective mean scores.

- There is one Independent variable with three or more (3+) categories. These levels are nominally scaled. (As a note, you can use an ANOVA to compare two groups, but the t-test is intended for that purpose.)

- There is one Dependent variable that is continuous in its numeric range. This means that interval or ratio scales are used.

- The statistic you obtain to determine statistical significance is the *F ratio* or F statistic.

- The Distribution Table in the statistics books or online is called the F distribution Table.

WALKING THROUGH THE STEPS FOR CONDUCTING A ONE-WAY ANOVA

An example will help to explain the basic purpose of the One-Way ANOVA.

Your school district has experienced a surge in student discipline offenses. As superintendent of schools you want to implement a Positive Behavior Intervention program at the elementary, middle and secondary levels in your district. However, the Board of Education will approve funds for only one during the upcoming school year. So you have to make a decision based on need. Where would the dollars best be allocated?

Step One: You state your null hypothesis.

There is no difference in student discipline offenses among elementary, middle and secondary schools in the district.

Step Two: You identify your independent variable and your dependent variable.

School type was your Independent variable with three categories—elementary, middle and secondary. You took the listing of your 39 classrooms and separated them by the three groups.

- Group One was the elementary school group with 12 classrooms;
- Group Two was the middle school group with 12 classrooms; and,
- Group Three was the secondary school group with 15 classrooms.

Using nominal scaling, you assign each classroom a numeric label so that your ANOVA could be calculated. You used 1, 2 and 3 as your numeric values which represented the three categories of the 39 classrooms.

Your Dependent variable was "Student Discipline Offenses." You listed the average number for each classroom. You also calculated the mean scores for each group (Figure 8.1). They appeared different, but you could not really tell until an ANOVA procedure was applied to the data.

	School Type	Group Code	Number of Student Disciplinary Offenses
1. Mrs. Polinsky	Elementary	1	123
2. Ms. Morelli	Elementary	1	119
3. Mr. Anderson	Elementary	1	120
4. Ms. Delgado	Elementary	1	103
5. Ms. Patel	Elementary	1	168
6. Mr. Dinh	Elementary	1	190
7. Mrs. Diaz	Elementary	1	120
8. Mrs. O'Brien	Elementary	1	130
9. Mr. Guzman	Elementary	1	103
10. Ms. Padilla	Elementary	1	104
11. Mr. Strada	Elementary	1	189
12. Ms. Hayes	Elementary	1	100
Group 1	**N=12**		**Mean=130.75**
13. Ms. Kinane	Middle	2	120
14. Mr. Calafiore	Middle	2	190
15. Mrs. Dean	Middle	2	189
16. Ms. Chai	Middle	2	145
17. Ms. Quinn	Middle	2	171
18. Mr. Bentur	Middle	2	189
19. Ms. Chaduri	Middle	2	145
20. Mr. Chung	Middle	2	177
21. Ms. Singh	Middle	2	189
22. Mr. Ross	Middle	2	167
23. Ms. Johnson	Middle	2	156
24. Ms. Mattiello	Middle	2	189
Group 2	**N=12**		**Mean= 168.92**
25. Mrs. Card	Secondary	3	120
26. Ms. Dombi	Secondary	3	134
27. Ms. Hodkoski	Secondary	3	155
28. Ms. Temkin	Secondary	3	134
29. Mr. Gavin	Secondary	3	144
30. Ms. Crovo	Secondary	3	133
31. Mr. Rae	Secondary	3	142
32. Ms. Perez-Bohn	Secondary	3	123
33. Mr. Amado	Secondary	3	110
34. Ms. Trinh	Secondary	3	102
35. Ms. Nulsen	Secondary	3	130
36. Ms. Schipul	Secondary	3	190
37. Ms. Trivella	Secondary	3	100
38. Ms. Rosenberg	Secondary	3	103
39. Ms. Reis	Secondary	3	120
Group 3	**N=15**		**Mean=129.33**

Figure 8.1.   Three Groups of Classrooms and Student Disciplinary Offenses for One-Way ANOVA

Step Three: You set up your data for data entry into a database.

The data for your One-Way ANOVA might be recorded in a database that looks like this. There are three sets of classrooms with a total of 39 (*N*). The groups are not exactly the same size, but close enough not to seriously violate assumptions of equal group size. The school type codes and the number of school discipline offenses are listed. Only those two pieces of data are entered into your statistical formula or statistical package.

Step Four: You execute the ANOVA statistical procedure to obtain an F ratio, the *calculated value*.

After you have entered your data from your database, you can execute the ANOVA. Whether you hand calculate the ANOVA or use a statistical package, the same result emerges—an F ratio. This is the statistic in ANOVA that indicates if you can reject the null.

Parallel to the t-test procedure, the F ratio is called our calculated value. It is usually a 3 to 4 digit number with two decimal places. The plus or minus sign does not matter; ignore it. For our data set, the calculated F ratio is 8.94.

Step Five: You compare your calculated F ratio to the *critical F ratio* in the F Distribution table using the correct degrees of freedom.

You have to compare your calculated F value to the critical F value, located at the end of many statistics textbooks or online. It is called the F Distribution Table. A portion of this is displayed in Figure 8.2. This is how you find the critical F value. You must use the Degrees of Freedom.

USING THE F DISTRIBUTION TABLE CORRECTLY: DEGREES OF FREEDOM

The degrees of freedom for ANOVA procedures are a bit more complicated and can cause some confusion. There are two numbers that compose your degrees of freedom for ANOVA: the Between Groups degrees of freedom (*df*) and the Within Groups *df*.

The Between Groups *df* is equal to the number of groups minus one (number of groups −1). In this case you had three school type groups. So your Between Groups *df* is 2 or (three groups minus 1).

The Within Groups *df* is equal to (the number in each group minus one [n − 1]), and then the *sum* for each group. In your case the Within Groups *df* is 36. It is calculated like this:

Group 1 [12 − 1] + Group 2 [12 − 1] + Group 3 [15 − 1] or
11 + 11 + 14 = 36

Between→

Within↓

DF	1	2	3	4	5	6	7	8	9	10
1	161	200	216	225	230	234	237	239	241	242
2	18.5	19.0	19.2	19.3	19.3	19.4	19.4	19.4	19.4	19.4
3	10.1	9.55	9.28	9.12	9.01	8.94	8.89	8.85	8.81	8.79
4	7.71	6.94	6.59	6.39	6.26	6.16	6.09	6.04	6.00	5.96
5	6.61	5.79	5.41	5.19	5.05	4.95	4.88	4.82	4.77	4.74
6	5.99	5.14	4.76	4.53	4.39	4.28	4.21	4.15	4.10	4.06
7	5.59	4.74	4.35	4.12	3.97	3.87	3.79	3.73	3.68	3.64
8	5.32	4.46	4.07	3.84	3.69	3.58	3.50	3.44	3.39	3.35
9	5.12	4.26	3.86	3.63	3.48	3.37	3.29	3.23	3.18	3.14
10	4.96	4.10	3.71	3.48	3.33	3.22	3.14	3.07	3.02	2.98
11	4.84	3.98	3.59	3.36	3.20	3.09	3.01	2.95	2.90	2.85
12	4.75	3.89	3.49	3.26	3.11	3.00	2.91	2.85	2.80	2.75
13	4.67	3.81	3.41	3.18	3.03	2.92	2.83	2.77	2.71	2.67
14	4.60	3.74	3.34	3.11	2.96	2.85	2.76	2.70	2.65	2.60
15	4.54	3.68	3.29	3.06	2.90	2.79	2.71	2.64	2.59	2.54
16	4.49	3.63	3.24	3.01	2.85	2.74	2.66	2.59	2.54	2.49
17	4.45	3.59	3.20	2.96	2.81	2.70	2.61	2.55	2.49	2.45
18	4.41	3.55	3.16	2.93	2.77	2.66	2.58	2.51	2.46	2.41
19	4.38	3.52	3.13	2.90	2.74	2.63	2.54	2.48	2.42	2.38
20	4.35	3.49	3.10	2.87	2.71	2.60	2.51	2.45	2.39	2.35
21	4.32	3.47	3.07	2.84	2.68	2.57	2.49	2.42	2.37	2.32
22	4.30	3.44	3.05	2.82	2.66	2.55	2.46	2.40	2.34	2.30
23	4.28	3.42	3.03	2.80	2.64	2.53	2.44	2.37	2.32	2.27
24	4.26	3.40	3.01	2.78	2.62	2.51	2.42	2.36	2.30	2.25
25	4.24	3.39	2.99	2.76	2.60	2.49	2.40	2.34	2.28	2.24
30	4.17	**3.32**	2.92	2.69	2.53	2.42	2.33	2.27	2.21	2.16
40	4.08	**3.23**	2.84	2.61	2.45	2.34	2.25	2.18	2.12	2.08
60	4.00	3.15	2.76	2.53	2.37	2.25	2.17	2.10	2.04	1.99
120	3.92	3.07	2.68	2.45	2.29	2.18	2.09	2.02	1.96	1.91
00	3.84	3.00	2.60	2.37	2.21	2.10	2.01	1.94	1.88	1.83

Figure 8.2.   F Distribution Table (partial table)

The degrees of freedom are these two numbers: 2 and 36. You will see it often reported like this ($df = 2, 36$). In order to use the F Distribution Table correctly, you have to know that the Between Groups df is reported horizontally across the top of the table, and the Within Groups df is reported vertically down the side of the table. So where these two numbers intersect in the F Distribution Table at your probability level of .05 or .01, there is your critical value. For $df = 2, 36$, the critical table value is between 3.32 and 3.23 in the table. For your data set, the calculated F ratio was 8.94. You exceeded or beat the table value.

Step Six: Accept or reject the null hypothesis.

Since your calculated value exceeds the critical value, you reject the null hypothesis.

There is a difference in student discipline offenses among elementary, middle and secondary schools.

Step Seven: You conduct follow-up tests to your ANOVA.

When you have statistical differences with t-tests, there are only two mean scores. You can look to see which is higher and which is lower, and then draw your conclusions and inferences. End of story. If you have a statistically significant result with ANOVA, your work is not complete. The only answer you have obtained at this point is that there *are* statistically significant differences among your groups—in this example, the three school types. But which groups are different on the variable of reading achievement? There are several possibilities where significant differences might exist.

- Between *Elementary*/A and *Middle* schools/B (A and B)
- Between *Elementary*/A and *Secondary* schools/C (A and C)
- Between *Middle*/B and *Secondary*/C schools (B and C)

With ANOVA there are more than two mean scores. You cannot eyeball the scores and make deductions. You have to conduct an additional statistical procedure.

A follow-up test, called a *post hoc* procedure, or multiple comparison test, is designed just for this purpose. It shows exactly where the significant differences lay after (post) a significant F ratio is obtained in ANOVA. It pinpoints which mean scores are significantly different from each other.

There are many choices for *post hoc* procedures to choose from. Each is named after the scientist who developed it.

- Fisher's LSD
- Duncan's new multiple range test
- Newman-Keuls

- Tukey's HSD
- Scheffe's test

Some are more conservative than others are, making it harder to reject the null. A liberal procedure will find a significant difference between two mean scores that are relatively close together. A conservative procedure will indicate that two mean scores are significantly different only when the means are far apart. From the list above, the Fisher LSD is the most liberal and the Scheffe's test, the most conservative.

You may wonder why t-tests are not used to compare each of the combinations above. That would be logical except for the fact that conducting multiple t-tests increases the chances of getting spurious results with error. As the number of t-tests increases, the probability of getting a statistically significant difference by chance alone also increases. This means you are approaching type I error territory! Multiple comparison tests adjust the level of significance to reduce the influence of chance results occurring.

For this example, you conduct a Scheffe's multiple comparison test. It showed that at the $p <. 05$ level our middle schools were significantly different from both the elementary and secondary schools on numbers of student disciplinary offenses. As superintendent of schools, you have decided to begin the program at the middle school.

REPORTING ANOVA RESULTS IN A TABLE FORMAT

Figure 8.3 shows how you might report your findings in a table format for your report to staff in your school system.

Student Disciplinary Offenses By School Type	Mean	(SD)	F ratio	df	*p*
Elementary School	131	(33)	8.94	2,36	.01**
Middle School	169	(23)			
Secondary School	129	(23)			

**p<.01

Figure 8.3. One-Way ANOVA Table

There are other more sophisticated ways to report ANOVA findings. You can find them in professional journals in different formats. However, for a lay audience, this is all you need to tell them. It makes the point and establishes where the focus should be for action steps in following up decisions based on data.

OTHER VERSIONS OF ANOVA

There are other versions of ANOVA procedures besides One-Way Analysis of Variance. These become more complex because of the added variables or factors in the research designs. If you are interested in using any of these, it may be wise to see a professional with expertise in multivariate procedures. There are multiple F ratios, interaction effects, and other aspects that make the following procedures more sophisticated both to execute and to interpret.

Factorial ANOVA

ANOVA designs called *factorial ANOVA*, compare more than one independent variable. Let's use the same example that we had in One-Way ANOVA, but add another independent variable, also referred to as a "factor." We subclassify our School Types into Subsidized Lunch—classrooms with 25% or more on subsidized lunch and classrooms with less than 25% on subsidized lunch. So, now we have School Type as one independent variable, and Subsidized Lunch as a second independent variable. Instead of three groups that we had in One-Way ANOVA, we have six groups because of the two independent variables. Sometimes, a design such as this would be listed as a 3 × 2 design. This means there are two Independent variables—one with three categories and one with two categories. Each of the six groups' mean scores on your one dependent variable of "Student Discipline Offenses" will be compared by the *Two-Way ANOVA* (Figure 8.4).

Elementary classroom 25%+ subsidized lunch	Middle classroom 25%+ subsidized lunch	Secondary classroom 25%+ subsidized lunch
Elementary classroom <25% subsidized lunch	Middle classroom <25% subsidized lunch	Secondary classroom <25% subsidized lunch

Figure 8.4.   2 Factor ANOVA: Type of School by Students on Subsidized Lunch Program

This can further become a *Three-Way ANOVA* by adding yet another in-dependent variable or third factor. Let's add "head of household." There are now three independent variables with twelve separate groups on which the dependent variable will be measured. The three Independent variables will have three categories (school type), two categories (subsidized lunch), and two categories (head of household). This may be called a 3 × 2 × 2 ANOVA design (Figure 8.5).

Elementary classroom 25%+ subsidized lunch Single Parent	Middle classroom 25%+ subsidized lunch Single Parent	Secondary classroom 25%+ subsidized lunch Single Parent
Elementary classroom <25% subsidized lunch Two Parent	Middle classroom <25% subsidized lunch Two Parent	Secondary classroom <25% subsidized lunch Two Parent

Figure 8.5 3 Factor ANOVA

ANCOVA

There is another very useful statistical procedure called Analysis of Covariance or ANCOVA. The purpose of this technique is to make groups equivalent before they are compared on the dependent variable.

As you may recall, one of the primary tenets of the t-test, as well as ANOVA procedures, is that the groups you are studying are alike *except* for your dependent variable. You want to insure that something else (called *extraneous variance* or *error*) does not account for differences between or among the groups. The ANCOVA adjusts for differences so that the focus of the analysis is the dependent variable and not error. Here is an example.

You are a reading specialist and have been awarded a grant to implement an innovative program called the Schoolwide Enrichment Model: Reading. One of your teachers implements the new program with her classroom, while another continues using the traditional program. When both classrooms are tested *before* the program begins, the results show statistically significant differences in reading levels between the two classrooms; the mean scores are statistically different.

ANCOVA is used to statistically equate the two classrooms' scores on reading before the innovation is implemented. This way the playing field is leveled and we can have a baseline that is similar for both classrooms. This allows us to determine whether a real difference occurred over time. ANCOVA determines if the instructional methods produce different results in reading skills, when the program is concluded, by equating the mean differences found at initial testing.

As a note, ANCOVA can be executed with two groups since the t-test does not have the capability to adjust for mean score differences. All ANOVA procedures, as mentioned before, can be done with two groups, if you wish, although most of the time a t-test better serves that purpose.

REPEATED MEASURES ANOVA

There are occasions when we need to measure something on a recurrent basis. You measure the dependent variable more than once; you repeatedly measure it. This is where the statistical procedure gets its name, *Repeated Measures ANOVA*.

For example, you may have a group of students whose writing skills you want to track for changes in proficiency levels. You test them in September, December and April, and again in June to determine their progress. Or you have a group of basketball players' free throw percentages you measure during the basketball season. Or you measure the level of teacher satisfaction with your school system in 2002, and every year afterward to monitor the ebb and flow. All of these occasions might lend themselves to using a Repeated Measures ANOVA procedure to determine changes over time and to track results.

CHAPTER SUMMARY

One-way ANOVA is a very useful statistic and a great partner to the t-test. It functions quite the same but affords us the opportunity to expand the number of groups beyond two. This is often called for in educational settings. The conceptual steps to ANOVA follow the t-test with the exception of the need to conduct post hoc tests after significant results are obtained. Many statistical packages offer this option as part of One Way ANOVA.

For statistical questions that are more complex (in that they add more dependent and independent variables to the research design), there are statistical models to accommodate them. Factorial ANOVA, ANCOVA and Repeated Measures ANOVAs are sophisticated statistical procedures that have been described in the most elementary fashion here. Reference to statistical or mathematical textbooks will present a detailed discussion. It may be wise to incorporate the assistance of someone with expertise in multivariate statistical analyses.

Chapter Nine

Chi-Square Analyses: Examining Distributions for Differences

NON-PARAMETRIC STATISTICS

In the previous two chapters, we discussed parametric statistics that answer questions about differences between groups (t-tests) and among groups (ANOVAs). Parametric statistics are of great value and used often in educational settings. Yet, one of the most valuable and popular statistics for educators is a non-parametric procedure called chi-square analysis. It is also called the test of "goodness of fit." Its symbol is x squared (x^2).

Unlike the t-test and ANOVA procedures, the chi-square is not as powerful to reject the null. It does not use the mean or standard deviation for computation; it does not rely on an interval or ratio scaling. Because the chi square relies on categorical or ordinal data, its value lays in the statistic's ability to answer questions about data that are nominal or ordinal. Variables in educational settings are measured very often by their categories—and not exact intervals. Chi-square allows you to answer important questions with variables measured with nominal or ordinal scales.

WALKING THROUGH THE STEPS FOR CONDUCTING A CHI-SQUARE ANALYSIS

A simple example of a chi-square analysis will promote the merit of this statistical technique. Let's say that your elementary school was concerned about the difference in math proficiency. The fourth grade classrooms had 50% males ($n = 40$) and 50% females ($n = 40$) or 80 fourth graders in all.

Step One: You state your null hypothesis.

There is no difference between male and female students on math proficiency, as assessed with a Common Core State Standards rubric. This null hypothesis sounds similar to the hypotheses for t-tests and ANOVAs, but there are no dependent and independent variables.

Step Two: You identify your two categorical variables.

The first is *gender* with two categories:

* male
* female

The second is *math proficiency* with four categories:

* Novice
* Apprentice
* Practitioner
* Expert

Step Three: You set up a Contingency Table of your Expected Frequencies

A *Contingency Table of Expected Frequencies* is an arrangement of your categorical data into a two-way classification scheme. One of the classifications becomes rows (across) and the other becomes columns (down). The boxes, formed by the intersection of rows and columns, are called cells. The cells tell us what you can expect, given the frequencies of rows and columns. It is a simple application of probabilities based on your sample numbers and their classifications. Figure 9.1 displays a Contingency Table of Expected Frequencies for your data.

Math Rubric Levels	Males	Females	**Row Classification**
Novice	10 (25%) Cell	10 (25%) Cell	20 (25%)
Apprentice	10 (25%) Cell	10 (25%) Cell	20 (25%)
Practitioner	10 (25%) Cell	10 (25%) Cell	20 (25%)
Expert	10 (25%) Cell	10 (25%) Cell	20 (25%)
Column Classification ↕	40 (50%) Cell	40 (50%) Cell	N=80

Figure 9.1. Contingency Table of Expected Frequencies

In the case of this example, the columns correspond to Gender with *two* categories. So you allocate two columns for each of the two gender categories. The rows correspond to the variable of Mathematics Proficiency and have *four* different categories. You allocate four rows for each of the four levels. You have 80 students altogether.

The classification for "columns" creates two categories of gender. Since there are 80 students, half of the students are males (40 or 50%) and half are females (40 or 50%). The "rows" for mathematics proficiency break into four categories. Since there are 80 students, the categories are: novice (20 or 25%), apprentice (20 or 25%), practitioner (20 or 25%), and expert (20 or 25%).

Then, you have to calculate the cells. The expected frequency of any cell in the table is found by multiplying the total of the column with the total of the row to which the cell belongs. The product is divided by the total sample size. So to obtain a cell for males, you multiple the total of the column (40) times the total of the row (20) and divide by 80, the sample size. You get 10 as your cell size. This is your expected frequency for each cell. It is helpful to report the cell size as well as its percentage. The Table for Expected Frequencies has both.

You have just constructed a Contingency Table of Expected Frequencies from the two nominal variables for your 80 students. Each cell has 10 students in it because of the breakdown of the two classification variables—gender and math proficiency (Figure 9.2). So what you would *expect* for your fourth graders as outcomes is that 10 females and 10 males will populate each of the four rubric classifications.

WHEN TO COLLAPSE CATEGORIES
TO MAKE CELLS LARGER

The table enables you to determine the nature of the relationships between your two categorical variables. As a recommendation, you should have at least five values in each cell. If not, it might be a good idea to collapse or combine a category in one of your variables in order to make the cell larger. This is important for statistical analysis with the chi-square. As an example, the categorical variable of ethnicity might reveal that the category of "Asian, African American and Native American" have only a few members each, while the category of white has many. You may want to create a category of "non-white" and "white" to increase the size rather than keep the three non-white categories, small.

Step Four: You set up your data for data entry into a database.

This is the list that you have been given. It indicates the math proficiency for your 80 students.

ID	Gender	4th Grader	Math Proficiency	ID	Gender	4th Grader	Math Proficiency
1	Male	Frank	Apprentice	41	Female	Krista	Apprentice
2	Male	Jose	Novice	42	Female	Felice	Apprentice
3	Male	Jacob	Novice	43	Female	Katherine	Apprentice
4	Male	Owen	Novice	44	Female	Martha	Apprentice
5	Male	Jack	Novice	45	Female	Olivia	Apprentice
6	Male	Robert	Novice	46	Female	Rita	Apprentice
7	Male	Bill	Practitioner	47	Female	Mande	Apprentice
8	Male	Mark	Practitioner	48	Female	Cindy	Apprentice
9	Male	Timmy	Practitioner	49	Female	Jewel	Apprentice
10	Male	Peter	Practitioner	50	Female	Yolanda	Apprentice
11	Male	Denzel	Apprentice	51	Female	Avital	Expert
12	Male	Charles	Apprentice	52	Female	Emily	Expert
13	Male	Roger	Apprentice	53	Female	Gail	Expert
14	Male	Joe	Apprentice	54	Female	Jeanne	Expert
15	Male	Angel	Apprentice	55	Female	Maura	Expert
16	Male	Craig	Apprentice	56	Female	Mary	Expert
17	Male	Peter	Apprentice	57	Female	Susan	Expert
18	Male	Guy	Novice	58	Female	Kerri	Expert
19	Male	Matt	Novice	59	Female	Cheryl	Expert
20	Male	Seth	Novice	60	Female	Ellen	Expert
21	Male	Tommy	Novice	61	Female	Mary Grace	Expert
22	Male	Mike	Practitioner	62	Female	Allison	Expert
23	Male	TJ	Practitioner	63	Female	Alyssa	Expert
24	Male	David	Practitioner	64	Female	Amelia	Expert
25	Male	Eddie	Practitioner	65	Female	Jennie	Expert
26	Male	Miquel	Practitioner	66	Female	Judy	Expert
27	Male	Drake	Practitioner	67	Female	Sandy	Expert
28	Male	Jesus	Practitioner	68	Female	Margaret	Expert
29	Male	Jim	Practitioner	69	Female	Polly	Expert
30	Male	Jeff	Practitioner	70	Female	Robin	Expert
31	Male	James	Apprentice	71	Female	Janice	Novice
32	Male	Al	Apprentice	72	Female	Julia	Novice
33	Male	Terry	Novice	73	Female	Charla	Novice
34	Male	Ray	Practitioner	74	Female	Amy	Novice
35	Male	Paul	Practitioner	75	Female	Annie	Novice
36	Male	John	Practitioner	76	Female	Estelle	Novice
37	Male	Barry	Practitioner	77	Female	Joanne	Novice
38	Male	Daniel	Practitioner	78	Female	Linda	Novice
38	Male	Zack	Practitioner	79	Female	Kateri	Novice
40	Male	Albert	Practitioner	80	Female	Margie	Novice

Figure 9.2. Data Set for Fourth Graders by Gender and Math Proficiency

You have decided to code gender:

- Male (1)
- Female (2)

Math proficiency has been coded:

- Novice (1)
- Apprentice (2)
- Practitioner (3)
- Expert (4)

The data set is scrambled. You decide to organize the data set dividing it into two separate groups: males and females. Then, you use the "sort" command in your word processing package to sort on the variable of math proficiency by gender. This is what the data now looks like—much more manageable. You can easily count the categories and their respective frequencies. This is a great time saver. For data entry, you will only use numeric data as Figure 9.3 reflects.

ID #	Gender	Math	ID #	Gender	Math
1.	1	2	41.	2	2
2.	1	2	42.	2	2
3.	1	2	43.	2	2
4.	1	2	44.	2	2
5.	1	2	45.	2	2
6.	1	2	46.	2	2
7.	1	2	47.	2	2
8.	1	2	48.	2	2
9.	1	2	49.	2	2
10.	1	2	50.	2	2
11.	1	1	51.	2	4
12.	1	1	52.	2	4
13.	1	1	53.	2	4
14.	1	1	54.	2	4
15.	1	1	55.	2	4
16.	1	1	56.	2	4
17.	1	1	57.	2	4
18.	1	1	58.	2	4
19.	1	1	59.	2	4
20.	1	1	60.	2	4
21.	1	3	61.	2	4
22.	1	3	62.	2	4
23.	1	3	63.	2	4
24.	1	3	64.	2	4
25.	1	3	65.	2	4
26.	1	3	66.	2	4
27.	1	3	67.	2	4
28.	1	3	68.	2	4
29.	1	3	69.	2	4
30.	1	3	70.	2	4
31.	1	3	71.	2	1
32.	1	3	72.	2	1
33.	1	3	73.	2	1
34.	1	3	74.	2	1
35.	1	3	75.	2	1
36.	1	3	76.	2	1
37.	1	3	77.	2	1
38.	1	3	78.	2	1
39.	1	3	79.	2	1
40.	1	3	80.	2	1

Figure 9.3. Data Set for Fourth Graders by Gender and Math Proficiency

Step Five: You set up a Contingency Table of your Actual Frequencies.

You are going to set up a table with your *actual* outcome data. The actual frequency data from your students creates the Contingency Table of Actual Frequencies. You look at your first Contingency Table of Expected Frequencies and then review the Contingency Table of Actual Frequencies (Figure 9.4). The cells appear to be statistically different, but you subject your data to statistical analysis—in this case a chi-square analysis. It is an exceptional statistic to determine if math proficiency levels for male and females are in fact different.

	Males	Females	Row Classification
Novice	10 (25%)	10 (25%)	20 (25%)
Apprentice	10 (25%)	10 (25%)	20 (25%)
Practitioner	20 (50%)	0 (0%)	20 (25%)
Expert	0 (0%)	20 (50%)	20 (25%)
Column Classification	40 (50%)	40 (50%)	N=80

Figure 9.4.   Contingency Table of Actual Frequencies

Step Six: You execute the chi-square statistical procedure to obtain *a calculated value.*

After you have entered your data from your database into the statistical program of your choice, you execute the chi-square procedure. You can also hand calculate the statistic by using a formula found in any statistics or mathematics textbook. Either way, after you execute the chi square statistical procedure, you obtain a Chi-Square of 40.00. This is called your *calculated value.*

Step Seven: You compare your calculated x^2 value to the *critical x^2 value.*

Next, you compare your calculated value to what is called the critical value located in a statistical table, called the chi square Distribution Table. It is displayed in Figure 9.5.

DEGREES OF FREEDOM

The degrees of freedom (*df*) for a chi-square statistic are calculated by taking (the number of rows minus 1) times (the number of columns minus 1). In the case of your fourth graders, you have two rows (Gender categories) and four columns (math proficiency). So the degrees of freedom equals $(2 - 1)$ times $(4 - 1)$ or 3.

df	Chi Square p<.05	Chi Square p<.01
1	3.84	6.64
2	5.99	9.21
3	**7.82**	11.34
4	9.49	13.28
5	11.07	15.09
6	12.59	16.81
7	14.07	18.48
8	15.51	20.09
9	16.92	21.67
10	18.31	23.21
11	19.68	24.72
12	21.03	26.22
13	22.36	27.69
14	23.68	29.14
15	25.00	30.58
16	26.30	32.00
17	27.59	33.41
18	28.87	34.80
19	30.14	36.19
20	31.41	37.57
21	32.67	38.93
22	33.92	40.29
23	35.17	41.64
24	36.42	42.98
25	37.65	44.31
26	38.88	45.64
27	40.11	46.96
28	41.34	48.28
29	42.56	49.59
30	43.77	50.89

Figure 9.5.   Chi-Square Distribution Table

$[2 - 1] = 1 \times [4 - 1] = 3$ or $1 \times 3 = 3$ degrees of freedom

If your calculated value exceeds the critical value in the statistical table, you reject the null. If not, you accept the null as true.

Step Eight: You accept or reject the null hypothesis.

For 3 degrees of freedom at the .05 level of probability, the critical chi-square table value is actually 7.82. It is shaded in Figure 9.5 so that you can see how it was located in the table. Since your calculated value for the chi-square is 40.00, you exceeded the table value. The expected frequencies were significantly different from what you observed to be true in your actual data. So you reject the null hypothesis.

There is a difference between male and female fourth graders on math proficiency.

REPORTING CHI-SQUARE RESULTS IN A TABLE FORMAT

From the study of fourth graders and math proficiency levels, you want to present the findings to the Board of Education and Parent Teachers Association in your school. Here is a simple format for reporting chi-square results (Figure 9.6). There are more sophisticated ways to report chi-square findings. You can locate them in professional journals. However, for a lay audience, this is all you need to tell them. It makes the point and establishes where the focus should be for action steps in following up decisions based on data.

4th Graders N=80	Frequencies/ Outcomes	Novice	Apprentice	Practitioner	Expert	Chi Sq
Males	Expected	10 (25%)	10 (25%)	10 (25%)	10 (25%)	40.00*
40=n	Actual	10 (25%)	10 (25%)	20 (50%)	0 (00%)	
Females	Expected	10 (25%)	10 (25%)	10 (25%)	10 (25%)	
40=n	Actual	10 (25%)	10 (25%)	0 (00%)	20 (50%)	

* p<.05

Figure 9.6.   Reporting the Chi-Square Results in Table Format

CHAPTER SUMMARY

The chi-square statistic, which relies on nominal and ordinal scaling described in chapter 1, is used heavily in educational environments. The chi-square statistical procedure allows us to compare groups against each other on important variables. Although it may not have the sophistication of its parametric counterparts, its utility may exceed theirs. It is a statistical technique that provides us with insights about students, schools and stakeholders that would be impossible to diagnose if you had to depend on statistics which required interval or ratio scaling.

Chapter Ten

Correlations: Detecting Relationships

Besides focusing on differences, many data-driven decisions are focused on relationships. There are times in educational settings where we wonder if two factors are linked. For example, we may ask some of the following questions:

- Does attendance in summer preschool increase kindergarten readiness?
- Does exposure to STEM careers increase interest in math and science?
- Does the use of technology increase math engagement in the classroom?
- Does exposure to classroom management strategies reduce student discipline offenses?
- Does performance on AP courses determine acceptance at selective colleges?
- Are paraprofessionals in the classroom supported by parents?
- Does daily writing in student journals increase reading comprehension?
- Can teachers' leadership skills impact the success of new teachers?

There are statistics that help to determine if relationships do exist, and if so, what the characteristics of those relationships are. This is where correlations are useful statistical techniques. They test the extent to which two variables occur together and how related they are. As statistics, correlations can be descriptive and inferential at the same time. They can describe your data and you can also infer relationships from samples to populations.

WHAT DATA YOU NEED TO PRODUCE CORRELATIONS

You need two sets of variables (or paired observations) on the same individuals. In correlations, the first variable is called x. The second variable is called y. Your data are paired observations of x and y on one person. You correlate x and y to see if there is a relationship. For the purpose of illustration, let's say that we wanted to know if physical fitness and weight were related for fifth graders. We thought if you were physically fit, you would weigh less. If you were in poor shape, you would weigh more. Fitness and weight would be our two variables for our paired observations. We would collect our data on all fifth graders. For each child, we would have weight (x) and fitness (y). Then we would calculate a correlation statistic and find the answer.

There are basically four conceptual areas that correlational procedures address. Each is followed by an example of variables that you might correlate with each other.

1. If one variable (x) *increases* does the other variable (y) *increase*? Example: greater parent-to-child reading time increases school readiness skills.

2. If one variable (x) *decreases* does the other variable (y) *decrease*? Example: chronic absenteeism reduces promotion to the next grade level.

3. If one variable (x) *increases* does the other variable (y) *decrease*? Example: increased after-school programming reduces discipline referrals.

4. If one variable (x) *decreases* does the other variable (y) *increase*? Example: Teacher satisfaction declines as the classroom size increases.

CORRELATION COEFFICIENTS (R)

The relationship between two variables, and the nature of that relationship, is measured by *a correlation coefficient*, symbolized by the letter r. A correlation coefficient is a two digit decimal such as $-.20$ or $+.78$. The numerical values can range from minus one (-1.00) through zero (0) to plus one ($+1.00$). However, -1.00 and $+1.00$ are perfect correlations; you hardly ever see these numbers in the real world. There is a formula for calculating a correlation coefficient; it is found in any statistical text. There are several versions, however. The different types are based upon the scales used in measuring your variables; they will be discussed shortly.

The correlation coefficient is a great statistic because a single number summarizes the *strength* and the *direction* of the relationship between two variables.

STRENGTH

The *actual numeric value* of the correlation coefficient tells us the strength of the relationship. The nearer the number is to either +1.00 or −1.00, the stronger the relationship is between the two variables. Correlations of −.88 and +.88 have the same strength. A correlation of −.88 is stronger than a correlation of +.87 by only an infinitesimal amount.

A zero correlation ($r = 0$) indicates absolutely no correlation whatsoever. The relationship between class size and teacher's salary would have no correlation ($r = 0$). Correlation of .07 or +.02 are negligible. Although there is no hard and firm interpretation of what constitutes strength, Table 10.1 presents some correlation coefficients with interpretation of strength suggested.

Table 10.1.

Correlation Coefficient	Strength
0	No correlation
±.01 to ±.30	Negligible to low
±.31 to ±.50	Low to moderate
±.51 to ±.70	Moderate to high
±.71 to ±.99	High to extremely high
±1.00	Perfect

CORRELATIONS AND SHARED VARIANCE

As a note, a correlation coefficient should not be interpreted as a percentage. Since it is a decimal, this can happen but is incorrect. If the correlation between teacher salary and level of teacher turnover is .50 (r), you cannot conclude teacher salary accounts for 50% of teacher turnover. You must square the correlation coefficient and multiply it by 100 to assess the *shared variance* of two variables. This is called a *coefficient of determination* (noted by r^2). For this example, 25% (r^2) is the shared variance between the two variables of teacher salary and turnover. You can conclude that 25% of turnover can be explained by salary. This coefficient of determination (r^2) is the percentage of variance held in common by the two variables. Table 10.2 indicates the correlation coefficients and the percentage of shared variance. As you can see, you must have an extremely high correlation to assume that two variables are part of each other.

Table 10.2.

Correlation (r)	Coefficient of Determination (r²)
.10	1%
.15	2%
.25	6%
.50	25%
.75	56%
.80	64%
.85	72%
.90	81%
.95	90%
.98	96%

DIRECTION

Relationships between two variables can be either positive or negative. That is what is meant by "direction." Therefore, correlation coefficients can be either positive or negative. A plus or a minus sign before the numeric value indicates direction.

If a correlation is positive, it means that:

- if one variable (x) increases, the other (y) increases, or
- if one variable decreases (x), the other (y) decreases.

Positive correlations sometimes have a plus sign before the decimal, but many times it is implied. So a positive correlation of +.67 might also look like .67.

If a correlation is negative, it means that:

- if one variable (x) increases, the other (y) decreases, or
- if one variable (x) decreases, the other (y) increases.

There is always a minus sign before the correlation to indicate a negative correlation. These are also called *inverse* correlations.

WALKING THROUGH THE STEPS FOR CONDUCTING A CORRELATION STATISTICAL TECHNIQUE

The following example will demonstrate the qualities of asking questions with correlational statistics. Let's say that you have 20 students in your eighth grade. As the building administrator, you believe that students who participate in after-school clubs and extracurricular activities have better attendance in school (Figure 10.1). You want to show that this is true because it can serve as powerful information for decision-making in your school with the Board of Education, with your professional staff, and with parents.

Step One: You state your null hypothesis.

There is no relationship between participation in extracurricular activities and school attendance.

Students	Attendance out of 180 possible days	Number of Extracurricular Activities
	X	Y
1. Alex	140	1
2. Jason	170	7
3. Alison	150	2
4. Amelia	135	2
5. Alyssa	160	5
6. Kerri	175	8
7. Ellen	160	6
8. Emily	155	3
9. Felice	165	8
10. Juan	135	2
11. Julia	180	8
12. Krista	165	7
13. Kara	145	3
14. Mark	140	3
15. Miguel	155	3
16. Craig	145	1
17. Olivia	175	8
18. Deanna	180	7
19. Rebecca	170	7
20. Seth	175	9

Figure 10.1.   Data Set for Attendance and Extracurricular Activities

Step Two: You identified your two variables, *x* and y.

Your variable *x* is the total number of days in attendance, as tabulated at the end of the school year. The variable *y* is the total number of after-school and extracurricular activities the child participated in during the school year.

Step Three: Set up your data for data entry into a database.

Step Four: You set up a *scattergram*.

Before you run your correlational procedure, you set up a graph of your data. As we learned with frequency distributions, graphing techniques can illustrate a message quickly and clearly. Similar to a frequency polygon, the scattergram is a graphic representation of your correlation data.

You start again with the vertical (ordinate) and horizontal (abscissa) axes on a graph. For your data set, you place the "number of club or extracurricular activities" on the vertical axis starting with 1 and ending with 10, a little above the highest value in your data set.

On the horizontal axis is the total number of days in attendance in the school year. Then, you plot variables x and y for each child on your graph. Place a dot on the graph where the two variables intersect. Figure 10.2 shows our scattergram.

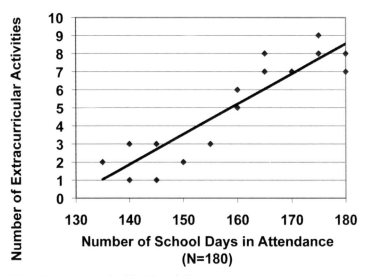

Figure 10.2.   Scattergram: Positive Correlation

WHAT SCATTERGRAMS CAN TELL US

Scattergrams are very useful because they tell a lot about our two variables and their relationship. Here are the pieces of information that scattergrams supply.

1. Scattergrams can *tell us the strength* of the relationship between the two variables.

- If the dots cluster close to an imaginary line, there is a very strong relationship or correlation between the two variables.
- When the dots are scattered in an ellipse or cigar shape, there is a moderate correlation.
- When the dots are scattered randomly around the graph, there is a low or negligible correlation.

In our scattergram, the dots are clustering close to an imaginary line or the line penciled in on the scatter diagram in Figure 10.2. We think that there might be a very strong relationship between the two variables. We have to execute a correlation statistics to truly find out, but the signs are there that a strong relationship exists.

Dots on the scattergram have another important function. Sometimes they are reviewed to determine the degree that one variable can predict the other. The more that the dots form that imaginary line or are cigar-shaped in an ellipse, the stronger there is prediction. In this case, the diagonal line through the spread of dots is called the "regression line" or the "line of best fit." The tighter the clustering of dots, the better one variable is at predicting another. In the case of our data set, the number of extracurricular activities might be considered a predictor of school attendance. The dots are clustered into a fairly tight line.

2. Scattergrams can tell us the direction of the relationship between the two variables.

- If the slope of the line falls from left to right, there is a negative correlation.
- If the slope of the line rises from left to right, there is a positive correlation.

The latter is the case with the data in our scattergram. The slope of the line rises from left to right signifying a positive correlation. The slope of the line indicates that as after-school and extra curricular activities increase, so does school attendance. Conversely, a positive relationship *also* means that as after-school and extra curricular activities decrease, so does attendance.

Just looking at the slope tells us a great deal about the relationship between these two variables.

3. Scattergrams can also show outlier scores. Observations completely out of range with all the others should be considered for elimination in the calculation of a correlation coefficient. They might contaminate the data set and give misleading results if a correlation coefficient is calculated. In our example, there are no outlier scores. All of our *x-y* intersections fall close to the line.

Figure 10.3 shows several scattergrams and the messages they convey.

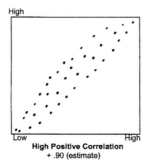

High Positive Correlation
+ .90 (estimate)

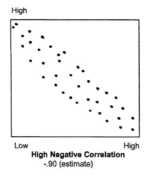

High Negative Correlation
-.90 (estimate)

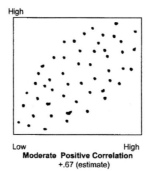

Moderate Positive Correlation
+.67 (estimate)

Figure 10.3. Scattergrams: Shapes That Depict Correlations

Step Five: You execute the correct Correlation statistical procedure.

You have looked at the scattergram and have a sense that a strong positive correlation exists between extracurricular activities and school attendance. Now, you want the statistical proof. You need to execute the proper correlation technique since there are many and the correct one should be selected carefully by characteristics in your data. The types of measurement scales for your two variables determine the type of correlation coefficient you use. This is where the awareness of scales, discussed in chapter 1, is so critical.

TYPES OF CORRELATION TECHNIQUES FOR CORRELATING TWO (2) VARIABLES X AND Y

- *Pearson Product Moment correlation* is a parametric statistic and requires interval or ratio data on both the x and the y variables to calculate it. This is the premier correlation statistic. As a parametric statistic, the assumptions of homogeneity of variance and normal distribution apply—just as they do with t-test and ANOVAs. Pearson Product Moment correlation is called Pearson r. We will be using this for our example since our data meet the measurement scale requirements.
- *Point biserial procedure* is a non-parametric statistic and uses a dichotomous, nominal scaled variable and an interval/ratio scaled variable to calculate it. An example might be correlating tardiness (late/on time) *and* frequency of behavioral problems in the classroom.
- *Spearman Rho* is a non-parametric statistic, which uses ordinal-scaled data with ordinal-scaled data for computation. It correlates two sets of ranks to determine their degree of equivalence. An example might be the relationship between students' satisfaction levels *and* their agreement with school policy on the use of cell phones on school grounds.
- *Rank biserial* is a non-parametric statistic and uses a dichotomous, nominal scaled variable and an ordinal-scaled variable to calculate it. An example is language spoken in the home (Spanish/English) *and* satisfaction with communication from school to the home.
- *Phi Coefficient* is a non-parametric statistic and correlates two dichotomous, nominally scaled variables. An example might be the relationship between gender (boys and girls) *and* participation in the athletics program (yes/no).

For our example, we used a Pearson Product Moment correlation coefficient and obtained a correlation coefficient of $r = +.78$. This is our *calculated* value. From the plus sign and from the size of the correlation coefficient we can immediately tell that we have a *strong, positive* correlation.

Step Six: You compare your calculated *r* value to the critical *r* value.

Next, you compare your calculated value to the critical value located in a Correlation statistical table usually found at the end of any research or statistics book or online. The degrees of freedom (*df*) for a Pearson Product Moment correlation statistic are the (number of pairs minus 2). In this case you have 20 pairs of data on students, so your degrees of freedom are (20 pairs − 2) or 18 degrees of freedom. You compare your correlation coefficient of .78 to the table value. It is .44 at the $p < .05$ level. You have a significant relationship between after-school/extracurricular activities and school attendance. *The Correlation Coefficient Table* (Figure 10.4) is displayed with the critical value in boldface to show how it is located in the table.

df	r p<.05	r p<.01	df	r p<.05	r p<.01
1	.997	1.000	24	.388	.496
2	.950	.990	25	.381	.487
3	.878	.959	26	.374	.478
4	.811	.917	27	.367	.470
5	.754	.874	28	.361	.463
6	.707	.834	29	.355	.456
7	.666	.798	30	.349	.449
8	.632	.765	35	.325	.418
9	602	.735	40	.304	.393
10	.576	.708	45	.288	.372
11	.553	.684	50	.273	.354
12	.532	.661	60	.250	.325
13	.514	.641	70	.232	.302
14	.497	.623	80	.217	.283
15	.482	.606	90	.205	.267
16	.468	.590	100	.195	.254
17	.456	.575	125	.174	.228
18	**.444**	.561	150	.159	.208
19	.433	.549	200	.138	.181
20	.423	.537	300	.113	.148
21	.413	.526	400	.098	.128
22	.404	.515	500	.088	.115
23	.396	.505	1000	.062	.081

Figure 10.4. The Correlation Coefficient Table

Step Seven: You accept or reject the null hypothesis.

Since your calculated correlation coefficient is .78, you exceeded the table value of .44 and can reject the null. There is a relationship between after-school/extracurricular activities and school attendance. Furthermore, the direction and strength tell you that as one variable increases so does the other. *Participation in these activities boosts school attendance.* Now, you have to determine how to get more students involved extracurricular activities in the future. You bring the information to your Board of Education, your professional staff, and your parents for their help and ideas.

SAMPLE SIZE AND SIGNIFICANCE OF CORRELATION COEFFICIENTS

As a note, the likelihood of obtaining a statistically significant correlation coefficient is based on sample size. If you have a large sample, you often have a significant correlation coefficient. For example, you can have 92 pairs of data and at the .05 level of statistical significance ($df = 90$) a correlation of $r = .21$ would be statistically significant. (Please refer to the table in Figure 10.4.) This is a low correlation! The *strength* of the correlation coefficient is much more important. Educators familiar with correlations will know this very important fact. Those who are less informed would use statistical significance to make their case, and it would be deceiving due to sample size alone. If there is an investment of time or dollars that hinges on the correlation, look at the strength of the correlation coefficient and pay much less attention to the asterisk (*) for significance.

REPORTING CORRELATION RESULTS

Reporting a correlation coefficient is very simple. Just use r and the equal sign. For example, for our data set we would report that there was a strong correlation between after-school/extracurricular activities and school attendance ($r = .78$). That is it. You may want to show your actual data set. The scattergram for illustration would highlight the impact that one variable had upon the other.

PRACTICAL APPLICATION OF CORRELATIONS

There are many uses for correlations that educators can avail themselves of.

1. The most useful purpose is to see if two variables are correlated. This is what chapter 10 has focused on.

2. Another important function of the correlation procedure is with respect to tests or instruments we measure with. The *reliability* of a test is reported as a correlation coefficient. It measures whether the test consistently measures what it purports to measure. You can be confident of that when you examine the correlation coefficient, reported in the test manual as the "reliability coefficient." If it is $r = .80$ or $r = .75$, we can be certain that it is a pretty reliable measurement tool. IQ tests have high reliability coefficients; Personality tests or Vocational Interest Assessments would have lower reliability coefficients.

3. A third function is performed by correlational statistics. If you are interested in determining whether two raters or two observers are seeing the same thing when they collect information, you are looking for inter-rater reliability. For example, if two of your teachers were evaluating the amount of time on task for the same group of students, you would want their observations (recorded by a checklist or rubric) to be very similar. By correlating their data, you would create an inter-rater reliability coefficient. Hopefully, the numeric value would be strong.

CORRELATING MORE THAN TWO VARIABLES

The possibility of correlating more than two variables is ever present in the education setting. However, this is where more complex statistical expertise is required. There are assumptions that must be adhered to in order to produce reliable and valid findings upon which decisions will be based.

When you correlate more than two variables you are undertaking a multivariate statistical analysis called *Multiple Correlation* or *Multiple Regression*. This technique can be used for prediction purposes and has been frequently used to predict college freshmen Grade Point Averages (College FGPA) with both forms of the SAT (Math and Verbal) and High School Grade Point Average (HSGPA). The formula below shows the prediction equation with the three predictors $[x^1, x^2$ and $x^3]$ and what is predicted $[y]$.

$$[x^1 \text{ (HSGPA)} + x^2 \text{ (SATM)} + x^3 \text{ (SATV)} + \text{constant} = \hat{y} \text{ (College FGPA)}]$$

There are two conditions that should exist when you use this multivariate technique:

1. The variables that you are using to predict with should have a low correlation with each other. In this case, HSGPA, SATM and SATV should have low inter-correlations. They are called the *predictor variables.*
2. The predictor variables, however, should have a high correlation with the variable that they are trying to predict, in this case College FGPA. This is called the *criterion variable.*

Please refer to other statistics books for in-depth discussion of Multiple Regression and other multivariate procedures.

CHAPTER SUMMARY

There is one last and very important point to make when correlations are discussed. No attempt should be made to say that one variable (x) causes the other variable (y). This is untrue. A correlation only suggests that a relationship exists between the variables. It does not mean that one variable causes the other. The use of correlational statistics is a great asset in educational settings. They suggest that relationships exist. To use them to pinpoint causality is a misuse of an unpretentious, but highly valuable statistical technique.

Chapter Eleven

Reporting Your Data Clearly and Strategically

Regardless of the relevance of the findings to the intended audience, the presence of data and statistics in a document is unappealing for most readers. Contemplating how the data look and how the message is delivered is important. This is particularly true if the report is directed at lay readers such as members of the Board of Education, parents, and community members. Most are not educators. Reports should be developed with the target recipients, first and foremost, in mind.

Here are some practical tips for formatting reports and presenting data. All of these points should be considered in advance or *a priori* of tackling the job. If you think out a plan in advance, it will eliminate a lot of stress when you are knee-deep in words and numbers.

Use a standard organizational framework to format your work. The document is the official record of your work. Its organization is important for telling your story (the results or findings) and for keeping readers connected to it. The reader needs to follow a logical sequence to understand the purpose of the study and how findings were arrived at. A well-constructed report will provide the reader with all of the necessary information:

Reasons for the research
Questions to be answered
Design strategy
Subjects and sampling procedures
Methods and procedures of data collection
Instruments selected to collect data
Findings (summary comments and recommendations)

This is the skeleton of any good story—a beginning, middle and an ending. A report should have the methodology in the beginning, what you found out in the middle, and what the results mean at the end. This is a logical thought process for any reader.

Keep the text concise and to the point. Most people reading your work do not want to spend a lot of time doing so. They want to get a handle on the findings and recommendations, and get on with their lives. Some writers tend to repeat themselves, making the same point over and over. Some bury a main finding in so much verbiage that the reader becomes confused, or misses it altogether. Sometimes two points are grouped together, also adding to confusion. If the point is worth making, the reader will pick up on it. As simple as it sounds, make your points one at a time. Keep the text simple, clear, and readable without run-on sentences and extraneous descriptive language. High-sounding language is not impressive and will only diminish the impact of your findings.

Use short sentences and simple points. Make the report straightforward. Boil it down, and then boil it down again. If the tables are well-conceived, a lot of narrative is unnecessary. Do not add educational or statistical jargon that the reader is unfamiliar with. If it is absolutely essential, make it user friendly by defining technical terms, otherwise, leave them out. This is neither a doctoral dissertation nor an academic journal article. It is roadmap for action to benefit your classroom, grade level, school, or school system.

Select a typestyle that is easy to read. Typestyles should facilitate the ease with which the reader is able to scan the page. This point sounds simple and is perhaps considered an unnecessary one to make. However, it is important that the document be viewed as inviting and easy on the eye. A difficult typestyle can detract from the content of the report. A report written entirely in italics or boldface will not be fully digested as opposed to a report written in Times New Roman. That is why most books are printed in this typeface.

Use boldface, italics, and uppercase, thoughtfully. There should be a reason why you shift from regular typeface to boldface, italics, and capitalization. A method to the madness should be evident. You may be making a point that needs special emphasis. You may be introducing a new concept or key word. You may be establishing an important header for change in narrative discussion. Whatever the reason, have one before you add these embellishments. If the reader does not immediately see the rationale, they may skip parts of the text.

Present tables to illustrate your findings. Tables can be your best friend in writing the main body—the findings. Usually tables are developed after the data are tabulated. This means that you have the tables to use when you tackle the narrative portion. Writing directly from the tables, generated by your work, will take the guesswork out of organizing the findings. It will be easy to present the findings logically in a way the reader can follow. Tables visually present a considerable amount of information to the reader in a way that can be readily understood. They allow the writer the opportunity to use a minimum amount of text to make key points.

Make the tables simple. Some tables are intimidating because of the large amounts of numbers they present to the reader. There is no way that most lay audiences can (or even want to) figure out what these types of tables represent. It is recommended that only one or two variables be presented in one table for a lay reader. This enables them to see your point, not be confused, and assimilate the message or finding. If you are reporting gender and grade levels, that is enough in one table. Instead of putting several variables in one table, use several tables to simplify the presentation. Keep that hat of the lay reader on your head.

Do not report numbers without percentages. In your tables that describe categorical variables or those variables with nominal or ordinal scales, do not list the numbers in each category without the corresponding percentages. With raw numbers only, you make the reader work harder. Again, make the data easy for them to grasp. Percentages convert raw data into meaningful information. The message is immediate and clear.

Include graphs if they add to comprehension of the findings. The prudent use of frequency polygons, histograms, bar charts, pictographs, pie charts and scattergrams is strongly urged. If they add to the story you are telling, put them in the report. If not, leave them out. Above all, use them if there is an inherent message that is conveyed. Do not add "so what" graphs; they waste the reader's time. Sometimes the sizzle of our computer capabilities overrides our judgement in the use of visuals. In a report of findings, they have less of a role. Their premier showcase is using them to make a visual PowerPoint presentation to an audience when the report is presented.

Interpret findings. One of the greatest challenges is interpretation of findings. What does this all mean? Do not assume that readers will be able to infer the practical implications of what you are reporting. Tell them. This will avoid confusion, frustration, and most of all misinterpretation of the results. Furthermore, tell the reader what action steps you feel are appropriate given the results. You do not need to call them "recommendations" if you feel that word is heavy-handed. You can simply list your suggestions. However, lay persons look to you for that insight. You are the experts in the educational arena. Even a few action steps, suggestions, or recommendations will give the report added weight and value.

Add an Executive Summary of findings. If you have a long report, it is likely that it will not be read by everyone (as tough as that realization is on our ego). So you want to provide a summary of your salient points. What do you want readers to remember? This is what constitutes an Executive Summary. As the report does, the Executive Summary should have a beginning, middle, and an ending. It should be broken down into sections with the use of bullets, boldfacing, or italics. The style should be readable, simple, and straightforward, as the whole report is. Encourage the reader to refer to the entire report if he or she needs to know more. Finally, this is the written document that will be disseminated and shared with the public, the media and many others. It needs to be carefully written so that it summarizes your findings thoroughly, honestly, and succinctly. Check for typos!

Provide a glossary of terms. Assume that the reader is unfamiliar with the field of education. Laypersons, including media professionals, will compose a sizeable portion of the reading audience for your work. It is safe to assume that most of them will be unfamiliar with the terms and programs that you refer to on an everyday basis. To make it easy for them, use a glossary to define terms or explain programs referred to. Avoid esoteric terminology and do not use abbreviations unless they have been defined in the glossary or already identified in the narrative. People who do not understand the terminology you are using without explanation will give up reading the document.

Ensure your report is read by an independent reviewer. This is the easiest thing to do in producing the final report and one of the most important. As writers, we have a tendency to get too close to our work. We may be too familiar with the subject matter or too impressed with our writing style. As a result, sufficient detail may be lacking in the explanation of some findings or too much abstract language used in others. An impartial reader who is aware of the intended audience can help to uncover flaws and alert you to areas where your readers may have difficulties or questions. Also, make sure that your report is well dressed. The adage that "perception is reality" is true. Typographical errors leave a bad impression and take away from your credibility. In the eyes of the reader, a carelessly compiled report can equate to a negligent and lax school system. If words are misspelled, or there are grammatical errors, this can only work against you—regardless of the quality of the report you are presenting. Have a colleague (as a critical reviewer) read your report before it goes to the public.

View the reading and listening audience with respect and dignity. There will be some who cannot sing your praises enough, and others who cannot sing your praises at all. Think about the people under the normal curve; these two small groups are the "tails. Those who disagree with your findings, or criticize some aspect of the study may even border on being picayune. As difficult as it may be, the respect and dignity of all consumers of public education must be respected. Listening to what lay persons say, honestly answering questions that you can answer and finding out information for questions you can't answer, go a long way in promoting your school. As educators, this approach is always a win-win even though it is tough-tough.

CHAPTER SUMMARY

Unlike many fads and trends in public education, *data literacy* is here to stay. This is because many decisions are based on systematically collected and compiled information. Data make for sound action steps. Yet the entrance of data has its price. It is more work, it is hard work, and it requires a commitment over time. The statistical procedures that are applied to the data sets must be selected carefully, planned wisely, and executed with at least a basic level of expertise. Statistics must be interpreted correctly, honestly and reported simply. Reports must make sense and be easily assimilated by lay audiences. But the price is worth it. Decisions based on data will represent a gigantic thrust forward in school reform and improvement for educators and stakeholders alike.